THE CRISIS IN THE CHURCH

A Semi-Fictional Dialogue

between

A Post-Vatican II-Evolving Catholic

James Marley

and an

Eternal-Doctrine Catholic

Ronda Chervin

BY

RONDA CHERVIN, PH.D.

PROFESSOR OF PHILOSOPHY AND

DEDICATED WIDOW

En Route Books and Media, LLC
St. Louis, MO

⊕*ENROUTE*
Make the time

En Route Books and Media, LLC

5705 Rhodes Avenue

St. Louis, MO 63109

Cover credit: Dr. Sebastian Mahfood, OP

Background image of the Vatican courtesy of Wikimedia

Queries may be sent to chervinronda@gmail.com

Library of Congress Control Number: 2020952264

ISBN-13: 978-1-952464-39-3

FOREWORD

I, the author of this book, Ronda Chervin, want you to know *The Crisis in the Church* is semi-fictional. I mean by this term is that what is totally real are the views expressed by Ronda in the dialogues. However, the names of places and thoughts of other participants, including the other dialogue partner, James Marley, are not factual.

The Crisis in the Church is more like a long op-ed than a scholarly book. Therefore, I have not included references to lots of other writers on the same subjects I have included or to prominent well-known speakers and writers about the crisis.

CONTENTS

1.

Introduction by Ronda Chervin

Why this book?

Because of the crisis in the Church, quite a number of books have been written by Catholic thinkers with the highest credentials about how to approach the rapidly growing divisions.

Now, it is not that I don't have credentials! With a Ph.D. in philosophy and an M.A. in Religious Studies; years of being a professor in universities and seminaries; and the publication of some seventy books, I am not exactly a Catholic who just happens to have a lot of opinions!

On the other hand, most of my books have been in the area of popular spirituality rather than academic theology, so any book I would write about the crisis in the Church will not be in the style of a professor of ecclesial history.

In fact, I have chosen to write my take in a rather breezy popular style. This is to appeal to concerned Catholics without higher degrees in philosophy or theology. On the breeziness, I thought such readers might find it intriguing that my semi-fictional dialogue partner is a man whose character and thoughts are based roughly on those of a widower whom I considered, many years ago, as a possible second husband for me, a new widow. I purposely picked out this person as a model for this present-day book to show how deeply rifts about the Church could sink a budding relationship.

I hope to include viewpoints on many sides of the divisions in the Church. I feel motivated to describe the ideas of those other than my own in a fair way, especially since lots of the anger and pain in today's Church is exacerbated by sarcastic ways of describing the views of opponents.

On the other hand, I will not conceal my convictions about the truths that I believe to be eternal and unchangeable.

2.

DAY I

The Dialogue Begins

(The setting of our encounter is St. Athanasius University in New York City in the summer of 2019.)

Here is the letter of invitation from the President of St. Athanasius:

Dear Doctorates from the year 1965 forward,

You all know there is a crisis in the Church. Many voices have been raised about the issues. There are more and more divisions. I have been thinking that a week-long seminar of some of the best minds in our Church, our Ph.D.'s in theology and philosophy, could lead to greater unity.

Please let me know if you can attend the Crisis in the Church seminar I am leading during the week of July 8-13 – Monday-Saturday noon. It goes without saying that we will provide room and board. Alcoholic beverages will be available at a small price at dinner.

May the Holy Spirit be with us.

[signed] Fr. Matthew Doria

MORNING SESSION:

(We began in the large meeting room of St. Athanasius University)

Ronda: (a short thin old woman in her early '80's, hair in a bun, wearing a jumper and Birkenstocks) Oh, my gosh, it's you, Professor James Marley, old pal and more!

James: (a large, portly, old man with grey hair and a medium sized beard dressed in a sports shirt and brown slacks) Glad to see you, Ronda. Please sit down next to me. I was hoping you would come.

Ronda: (Grinning) You know, even though we were at such different poles of the Church, when I became a widow and you became a widower in the '90's, I actually thought we might become wife and husband!

James (smiling): I remember, of course. It was a fascinating fantasy…You may not know that I did remarry, but to a woman friend who agreed with my points of view on the Church.

Ronda: Oh, I didn't. Is she here?

James: No, she's home. Her daughter is taking care of her while I'm at this seminar.

The author, Ronda Chervin, ever ready for dialogue.

Ronda: By the way, the reason I am wearing this dull blue jumper and white blouse, instead of the Hawaiian moo-moo's I used to wear when you knew me well, is because I am now a dedicated widow – like a consecrated widow – with a private promise not to re-marry and live only for Jesus and the Church.

James: I am delighted you have found a good path.

James Marley, Ronda's interlocuter.
Photo by Mathias Konrath - Unsplash

First Introductory Talk

Fr. Matthew Doria: (a tall, heavy-set man of about 65 years with a round face and curly grey hair.)

"With God all things are possible!" (Matthew 19:26)

"The gates of hell will not prevail!" (Matthew 16:18)

Fr. Doria

https://pixabay.com/photos/priest-mass-roman-catholic-faith-81872/

Let us pray: Jesus, You wanted us all to be one. Here is your Church of the 21st Century so divided! Please bless this seminar with Your truth that transcends all divisions.

Before describing the divisions in the Church of our time, I would like to point to what we all still have in common as Catholics:

1. We all believe in the existence of a personal God.
2. We all believe in the Trinity.
3. We all believe that while on earth Jesus initiated an ecclesial body called the Church.
4. We all believe that Jesus works through Word and Sacrament.

I would venture to say that anything else one of us believes might be doubted by someone else in this very room.

I will not ask you to raise your hand and propose something besides these four because I don't want us to begin with argument...oops, argument itself is a politically incorrect word – we need to say discussion – and even that offends some ears these days – would pleasant sharing be better?

(Laughter)

During the daytime we will have group sessions here in the meeting room. Meals will be in the cafeteria. In the evenings we will have healing sessions in the chapel. There will be Mass every day at noon.

Now, many would say that one of the key steps to overcoming division is the unfortunate habit some of us have of caricaturing our opponents. At the risk of falling into that trap myself, I think it will be helpful to propose, for the dialogues we will soon engage in, a tentative spectrum of divisions.

You might be surprised that I don't simply divide the Church into liberals and conservatives. There is a good reason. Those terms are political. When transferred to talking about the Catholic Church they can appear to be describing simply a general way of thinking about values. However, in the Church the issue of the truth of what is being taught is key.

When I sent out letters of invitation to you Ph.D.'s, one wrote back: "The Roman Catholic Church is a very big tent. Some Catholics find themselves on the traditional or conservative end of the spectrum, other Catholics find themselves on the modern or liberal end of the spectrum. Most Catholics live somewhere along the spectrum. All are Catholic. You are Catholic. I am Catholic. Let's just acknowledge our unity and not dwell on the differences."

That would be fine if we were talking about something like tastes in clothing. However, division-causing statements in the Church do not simply reflect a general way of thinking but a specific idea about whether a certain doctrine is true, false, or in need of evolution.

The Spectrum I will now present reflects the reality of Church issues that have enormous impact.

Fr. Doria handed out a sheet with this Spectrum on it so we could refer to it throughout the week.

1-5   Spectrum

(Note, these descriptions are just about issues that divide - they don't pretend to encapsulate the whole Catholic life of those who fall into them.)

1. Radical Progressives: We think there ought to be women priests, sacramental marriages of same sex couples, and we are often pro-choice. Most of us think the Catholic Church is not the only true faith, but only one of many good religions. On politics, many of us think there should be no borders between countries.

2. Post Vatican II - Evolving Catholics: We think the same way as those #1's about some of those items such as women priests, but not all of them. We think that some moral teachings should evolve with the times. The stances of Pope Francis have given us hope for the Church of the future. On immigration, most of us think there ought to be no border restrictions except for criminals, and most of us won't vote for any Republican, even if Democratic candidates are pro-abortion. We are for most economic justice initiatives.

3. Moderates: We are those who some, on each end of the spectrum, would call moderates. And both sides sometimes are angry at us for not siding with them against their opponents!

Most of us agree with the moral teachings of the Church, but many of us think that penalties for disobedience need to evolve somewhat with the times. Instead of leaving the Church over scandals, we think all Catholics should be part of the reform through a deeper Catholic life. On politics we think there needs to be a border, but most immigrants should be helped as needed. Some of us vote Democratic and some Republican or for small alternate parties.

4. Eternal Doctrine Catholics: Many of us think there is already an irreparable division in the Church because some Bishops believe false teachings and some are complicit in certain sins and/or cover-ups of scandals. Many of us would welcome the retirement of Pope Francis. We think many priests never teach some of the harder moral doctrines because they don't believe them totally and/or fear losing members of the congregation if they teach them. Some of us agree with all of the above but don't tend to relate to anything with anger, taking more of a spectator view. Some think the Tridentine Mass is always to be preferred even if the English Mass is valid. Politically, even though most of us think amnesty for illegal undocumented workers who were fleeing political tyranny is good, we are for greater restrictions on immigration designed to keep out drug dealers and sex-traffickers.

5. Traditional Catholics: Some of us think there is already a schism in the Church that is inevitable. Some only go to Tridentine Latin Masses even if they think the English Mass is

valid. Others think the traditional Latin Mass is the only valid Mass. Most think Holy Communion in the hand is a sacrilege. Some think that all supposed Popes after Pius X are anti-Popes. We think we are the true Catholics.

As you can readily see, in this spectrum, politics and religion intermingle a lot because those who champion economic justice are usually democrats and pro-lifers usually Republicans.

Now, I would like the 25 or so of you who came for this seminar to divide into groups of four or fewer at the tables provided and talk to each other for about an hour concerning the questions on the page headed Session 1. You can grab snacks and beverages on your way.

These will be your groups for the entire 5 weekdays. Saturday will only be a half-day. I would hope that you would want to sit with participants whom you don't know very well. Especially, don't sit only with those you know are the same number on the spectrum. Our goal is ameliorating divisions in the Church right here!

Just as Fr. Matthew's introductory remarks ended to polite applause and some laughter, James Marley's phone started vibrating and, after checking who was calling, he left the area. Wanting very much to be at a table with my old friend, James, I, Ronda, waited for him to come back to choose a group. But when he returned after 10 minutes, all the 6 tables had 4 people at them. So, I asked James if he would mind being in dialogue just with me for this week. (Of course, he agreed!)

When we picked up coffee and donuts and seated ourselves at a table, here is the dialogue that followed:

Ronda: No emergency, I hope??

James: No, my wife's daughter needed to find the credit card to do some shopping.

Ronda: (opens her seminar folder to the page marked DAY 1) Let's see what the plan is.

Questions for Group Sharing:

1. Where do you fit on the Spectrum of categories of Catholics 1-5? (Many Catholics don't fit neatly into any of these 5 categories. They have a mixture of things they agree or disagree about in Church teaching without fitting into a pattern. If you are one of these, when you talk about where you fit in the spectrum, just explain what you identify with in any of them.)

2. Each seminar participant will now have a turn to tell the others about your Catholic background (baptized as a baby, convert, revert returning to the Church after a hiatus, etc.) and what your family was like, as in strong, daily Mass Catholics; strong, faithful Catholics going to Church every Sunday and Holy Days; somewhat faithful Catholics; one parent practicing and receiving Communion and the other not; your children going

to Catholic schools, and so on. If you are not finished with this by lunch-time, continue this afternoon so each one has a turn.

Noon Mass

1 PM Lunch and Rest

2 PM Prayer in Adoration Chapel

3 PM Afternoon Session

Continue with any sharing not finished in the morning session and then respond to question 3.

3. Talk about how your views about the Church developed during graduate school and in your work settings and ministries.

5:30 PM Dinner

6:30 PM Healing Session

Ronda: Okay, let's look at Question 1. What type in that Spectrum did you identify with, James?

James: I would certainly describe myself as a type 2.

Ronda: And I would identify with type 4....Do you mind telling me

which of the things under type 1, Radical Progressive, you do agree
with even though you don't identify with the whole category?

James: Not at all. I agree there should be women priests. About same-
sex unions, I think they should be blessed but not called marriages, but
I am absolutely pro-life. Still, I could never vote for a Republican who
is pro-life but has no heart for the poor. If you recall, I am a both-and
person…you are more an either-or person.

(James was referring to a distinction made in philosophy, originally
based on the contrast between Hegel and Kierkegaard. Where Hegel
saw the history of thought involving a thesis, an antithesis, and a
synthesis (both-and), Kierkegaard thought we need to choose between
ultimate values in an either/or manner.)

Ronda: I'm glad to hear you are pro-life…you know that is my big
issue and for 30 years I prayed and talked to women in front of
abortion mills to tell them how we could help them.

James: I do remember. I admired you for that…Well, that said, let's
look at sharing question 2.

Ronda: You know a lot of my background, of course, but it's been so
long you may need a brief reminder. So, I was brought up as a total
atheist whose parents met in the Communist party, but then became
anti-Communists. I looked for truth in philosophy but in my non-
religious colleges only found skepticism and relativism. I looked for
love in affairs but these relationships produced despair. By 20, I

thought it better to commit suicide if all there was in life was suffering…

(At this point James, took my hand and gave me that empathetic glance with his large blue eyes I had loved so much when we were seeing each other in the '90's.)

Then the miracles happened that led me into the Catholic Church with the help, also, of great books in defense of Christianity such as those of C.S. Lewis and of the Catholic Church, especially those of Chesterton and Cardinal Newman. At 21, I became a daily Mass Catholic.

James: Of course, my story is much less dramatic. I was brought up in a French-Canadian ancestry family in Louisiana. My parents were faithful to all the teachings of the Church and all its practices. Curiosity about the North and about life in New York City led me to St. Athanasius where I majored in philosophy at the college level and stayed to finish my doctorate in theology. And I have been teaching here at St. Athanasius ever since!

With almost an hour before Mass, while those at the other tables took their turns sharing, James and I spent the remaining time with my catching him up on my numerous teaching and ministry jobs after we drifted apart in the '90's.

THE MASS:

Our family having moved to the suburbs after my Ph.D. studies, I was rarely at the chapel at St. Athanasius. It was moving to me to see Fr. Doria, my beloved University President, now so much older but still the same in many precious ways.

Without being casual, he intoned with warmth the words of the more than 2,000 year-old ritual. At the Consecration, I could still see the expression of rapt awe in his face that used to lift me out of my usually distracted thoughts.

The peace gesture of the congregation was also warm even though most of us didn't know each other coming from graduations during different decades of the 20th and 21st centuries.

In Fr. Doria's homily, the thing that stood out most for me were his remarks about Jesus being the "Way, the Truth, and the Life." He quipped in his usual funny way, "Of course, each of you noble professors tend to think that your own teachings are the Way and the Truth…at this seminar, however, we need to open ourselves to the presence of Jesus so we are not only exchanging our own concepts. Ask Jesus to come into your prayer time in a special way at Adoration before the afternoon session.

LUNCH:

Obeying Fr. Doria's insistence that we sit with other participants during lunch than the ones in our session group, I joined a table with much younger Ph.D.'s, all now professors teaching in many different areas of the United States.

We began by introducing ourselves, telling when we were in the Ph.D. program at the university and where we had taught since.

After that, here are some of the things said around my table:

"Well, we know we're all here because we love Fr. Doria – such a teddy-bear priest, warm, round, affable, and he probably helped all of us through hard times during our doctoral studies, but...I don't really like being shoved under these numbers in that Spectrum of his!

"I do love Fr. Doria, and that's why I would never call him a teddy-bear priest. That's so disrespectful!!!

"That Spectrum gives me the feeling of them vs. us that in itself represents a Church divided!"

"Father Doria said we all believe in the Trinity, but I read in a liberation theology book that some think Mary is the Fourth Person of the Godhead!"

"I bet there are no 1's and 5's here – because they don't believe in dialogue with those totally on the other side. Maybe all 2's and 4's are here mainly to influence the moderates?"

"Should we leave the last day with T-shirts imprinted with the Spectrum and our number with a check on it?"

"I wonder where Fr. Doria puts himself in that spectrum??? Where would you all put him?…

"Just a little point here – even though moderates are usually not angry about the divisions of the Spectrum, we are sometimes angry that others are angry!"

ADORATION:

After a nap, I went to the dear old chapel for Adoration prayer. I like to joke that the set-up of Adoration with the large Eucharistic host on the altar is good for me because Jesus is the center, not me!

Almost all the participants came to Adoration. It was moving to see them not talking but in deep prayer.

In my heart I asked Jesus: "Why am I afraid to be in this seminar?"

He seemed to reply with inaudible words, "Because you think that your opponents in the Church are nibbling away at your life-raft. But they can't. I am the Way, the Truth and the Life, and I will be victorious."

AFTERNOON SESSION:

When I came back to the auditorium to look for James, he had the schedule open at our table.

> How did you see these divisions developing in the course of
> your work as a theology or philosophy professor and/or in
> your ministries?

James: I'd like to begin. I find that those unfamiliar with Church history, as I studied it as a theology grad student, don't seem to realize that there have always been divisions in the Church. You need only think of the Arian heresy, where most of the Bishops disagreed with what became the official teaching about the nature of the 2nd Person in the Trinity. Or think of the Illuminati at the time of St. Francis with their exaggerated strange ideas about marriage; or those Jansenists with their rigorist way of making optional choices into absolutes, challenging the Jesuits, who were then mostly very lax; followed by modernism in the Church fought against by Cardinal Newman.

Ronda: When I was researching the great women saints and mystics I was amazed to read that there were actually saints backing different alleged Popes in the time of Avignon where St. Catherine of Siena persuaded one of them to return to Rome!... And, of course, a division that is not in Fr. Doria's Spectrum would be all those non-practicing Catholics whom Protestant Churches boast of having taken over!

But, of course, it's different to read about these past divisions than to experience them at the universities where we teach and to see them dividing our own families.

James: Now, I remember telling you years ago about my substantial on-site research into Native American religion and later, Islam. My life as a professor and theological writer greatly expanded my understanding of the insights of these religions. Not to diminish my love of our Catholic Church, but to lead me away from the kind of triumphalism so current before Vatican II.

(For any readers unfamiliar with that term, triumphalism is taking inordinate pride in the success of a political party or religious institution.)

I mean we used to talk as if the Catholic Church had all the truth, and other religions were simply bogus.

Ronda: My experience was so different. I had studied Catholic philosophy with the great Dietrich Von Hildebrand. Right after Vatican II, I started reading the *National Catholic Reporter* and hearing that there were theologians who thought the Church would change its position on contraception.

I was veering toward what Fr. Doria would call a Moderate Catholic position, open to evolution in Church moral teaching. But, then, Von Hildebrand wrote his thunderous refutation of such divergence under the title *The Trojan Horse in the City of God*. After that, his disciples started reading *The Wanderer* or the *National Catholic Register*.

Then, when I began teaching ethics myself at St. Paul's College in New Rochelle, I was appalled to find that the priest chaplain would tell couples that if they loved each other sex before marriage was okay. A priest told one of my students that "Dr. Ronda is only a lay person. What does she know!"

Three months later, that unmarried couple was planning to abort their newly conceived baby because it would wreck up their college plans to have a baby just then. The priest seemed totally surprised that this could happen.

I talked them out of it and loved to see the young woman with that baby in a stroller bringing him to classes and witnessing in that way to her pro-life decision!!!

I went through years of opposition from other philosophy faculty at St. Paul's. I responded by writing my own ethics book *Living in Love: About Christian Ethics.*

By the time I retired 3 years ago, I had taught several generations why Catholic teaching is so true.

James: Let's dialogue about those issues as we come to them in the days to follow. Fundamentally, I doubt that I disagree with you about moral teachings, but more that I think the root cause of choosing the wrong path is not lack of understanding but more lack of a deeper spirituality.

Right now, I'd like to hear more about your book about the Widow

Saints I noticed in the library this afternoon.

Before dinner, Fr. Doria came around to make this announcement: Please, try to sit with those you didn't meet at the 2 Sessions or at lunch. Also, I would like you to share about incidents that happened or you read about which gave you a new perspective on something involving Church issues.

There are drinks available at the small bar in the dining room. A senior at the college agreed to serve in exchange for free drinks for himself!

(Laughter)

DINNER:

Hmmmm, I thought. Ask for a Bloody Mary, a drink I used to have with my husband on occasion? Or, just get a Coke so I won't possibly scandalize anyone as a Dedicated Widow in this pseudo-nun looking outfit needing to drink?

I compromised by selecting a small bottle of wine.

Alas, at 82 it is hard for me to open such a bottle. One of the young woman professors took it off my hands. It gave me the opportunity to share my favorite aging maxim:

"When I can't do something like open a bottle or lift a parcel, I say to myself 'Well, Ronda, if someone offered you $500 to figure it out, could you do it?' It works like a charm! Within five minutes, I've solved the problem, but since you are so young and strong, I will just let you help me."

When we got around to sharing about surprising incidents which helped us with division in the Church, here are some of the ones I liked:

"I just happened to read a memoir of an Episcopal pastor of the 1920's in the U.S. Now, I always thought of Episcopalians as being kind of a mediocre compromise between Catholic and Evangelical, but this author sure changed my mind. He had an incredible ministry to the poor. Even if there was a huge snow storm, he would ride through the night to reach some poor woman expecting a baby, bringing the family their first real stove. He was belittled by high Church Episcopals for providing free dinners at every service instead of stressing only worship."

Another participant told this anecdote: "I was arguing with another professor about Church divisions. She suddenly said, "You don't think that theology professors will save the Church do you? The anawim (the poor, uneducated) will save the Church!"

HEALING SESSION:

Fr. Doria: Now dear Ph.D.'s I want to lead you in a healing session. I have spent many hours in Adoration prayer composing these reflections and exercises.

After all, in this seminar, I am not trying to hone up your skills as debaters, but rather as lovers of Christ in the Church.

However, I realize that some of you #4's will think that even talking about healing is a covert way of trying to make it seem as if divisions could be sugar-coated simply by becoming a "nice" tolerant Church.

Not really! I guess you wouldn't have come to this seminar unless you trusted me to surprise you!

Let us begin with prayer:

Holy Spirit pour out your gifts upon us, especially the gift of wisdom. Overcome with forgiving love, anger coming from wounds attributed to opposition from those in other parts of the Spectrum.

(Fr. Doria looked around at the mostly skeptical faces of his graduate students.)

Impossible? Come on! How many of you saw the movie *The Passion*?

(Many raised their hands.)

If Jesus could forgive those torturers and the leaders that arranged for His Crucifixion, who could you not forgive?

Now, don't think I am asking you to renounce the truths you hold after many years of thought to get to some phony unity. My hope is that each of us may be enlightened in a new way by our dialogues. But, also, that there would less anger even when we disagree.

Surely none of us Catholics are hoping for a time when every major disagreement leads to a new schism until one day we are like the 40,000 divisions of the non-Catholic Christian Church!

(Laughter)

We will be offering sacramental confession in the chapel area starting at 8 PM. Two priest friends of mine have agreed to be there, and I will also be hearing confessions.

The audience in rapt attention during Fr. Doria's healing service.
https://www.flickr.com/photos/catholicpress/9193674706/in/photolist-EkUxWC-S5EkK5-
ER3ZtW-FiC8RF-FiC7Lz-FadGiX-ER3Xvs-ER3WUN-EmfriX-EmfqYZ-ER3VNQ-
F7VVD1-F7VVgN-FiCaqn-S5Em5J-S5Embq-S5EkZd

I noticed that quite a few participants who looked wary when Fr. Doria started speaking, now looked more relaxed with hands loosely in their laps instead of crossed across their chests.

Fr. Doria then began to speak of the theme of this evening's healing service:

As you all know, I have been teaching Catholic Anger Management for many years. One of the theories I have taken over from non-religious counsellors is that underneath anger is fear.

How so? Consider this scenario. It is winter and the windows of the car are closed. Even though the bad driver who has greatly angered a man on his way to work can't possibly hear him, our hero is yelling curses at the man at the wheel in the speeding car.

Can you see that underlying the cursing driver's rage is the fear that such drivers can often cause death-dealing accidents on the road?

By contrast, I was told by a car-pooler that one of our professors here at St. Athanasius actually prayed aloud for every bad driver he passed!

Now, the analogy. A Catholic leader, a #4 on the Spectrum, is enraged by reports of priests involved in scandalous sins with minors. Our leader often imagines what these might have been, glad to read more and more of the explicit accounts. She's enraged to read about cover-ups, past and present-day.

What is the fear behind the anger?

Probably it would be some of these:

My son or grandson might go through this sexual abuse? It might even lead him to become a pederast one day!

Do I have to home-school my male children because I don't trust even the parochial school I have been sending them to?

If I can't possibly know the truth about allegations concerning priests, how do I know I am not shunning a priest who is really innocent?

Now let's look at the anger and fear of a #2 Post Vatican II Catholic.

A music minister in a parish is angry at the new Pastor. The choir director has been working with the singers and the parishioners to build up wonderful weekend Masses with almost everyone actively participating.

He remembers with horror how in the past he could see rows of old ladies praying the rosary during the Mass only joining in an Ave Maria hymn occasionally. By the way, I eventually came to understand these old women. I think the rosary at Mass functions as a mantra, but also to keep nervous fingers from picking at their nails when unoccupied. Back to our music minister: now the new pastor is insisting on a Latin High Mass every Sunday. "He had the nerve to ask me if I would like to take an on-line course in Gregorian Chant!"

What is the fear underlying the choir director's anger?

In six months, this priest may hire someone else to take my place!

This parish could be taken over by those fanatical Rad Trads! Our Bishop may have put this priest in precisely to bring about such changes.

So, what is the answer? Anger? Fear? Or…….??????????

Before offering healing meditations I would like each of you present tonight to silently answer this question:

> What I am most angry about that Catholics in other places on the Spectrum than my own have done or said? (Take 10 minutes to answer this or explain why you are not angry when others are.)

The auditorium become completely silent.

I, Ronda, thought about how angry I was when other professors at my Catholic College taught the students in ways opposite to what I was teaching. One that got me angrier and angrier is the subtle assumption some made that all religions are good so we don't have to evangelize. Now, please take another 10 minutes to try to see what the fear behind your anger is.

If you are not angry, review what gifts of nature or graces you have received that keep you serene when you experience or undergo injustice.

At first, I, Ronda, was not sure what the fear was. Then I got it. Of course, I am afraid of having less and less Catholics. I am afraid they will leave for another religion just because something there was appealing to them, such as Transcendental Meditation. I could wind up being in a tiny minority Church like the Amish!

Fr. Doria: Now I will present a healing prayer about anger and fear. As I speak, you insert into it the people who have angered you and your own fears. If you are not angry, use this time to pray for those who are.

Since you are all Catholic scholars, you surely have heard of St. Augustine's famous maxim: "Hate the sin, love the sinner."

Now, each one think of that thing in the Church you feel most angry about.

Now talk to Jesus and tell Him about your anger – take about 5 minutes to do this….

I, Ronda, spoke to Jesus about my anger at those who don't think that the Catholic Church is the one true Church and that others are just as good.

Fr. Doria: Now try to imagine what Jesus might be telling you about

His anger about the same thing. Of course, you are all sophisticated enough Ph.D.'s and professors to know that we are not to take such inner messages as infallible...but that doesn't mean that Jesus doesn't want to talk to us this way either!

To use the examples I told you about with a #4 and a #2, Jesus might tell you in your heart something like:

> If you are scandalized about priests abusing boys, think how I feel! I chose this man to be a priest and have given him enormous graces to overcome sinful tendencies and then he turns his back on Me and gets into evil, harms little children, and is also a great failure in his vocation.

In the case of the choir director, Jesus might say something like this:

> In My time rabbis sang their teachings. I love to hear a whole Church full of people singing loudly whether it is in Latin or the vernacular of each country. I am sad that your good initiatives are at risk.

Of course, I realize that some of you are not accustomed to hearing "words in the heart" when you pray. Try to open yourselves to that possibility tonight, but if that doesn't come now, ask the Holy Spirit to enlighten your minds with good thoughts of your own.

When I, Ronda, asked Jesus what He thought about our Church vs. other religions, He seemed to teach me "I formed the Catholic Church. It is Mine. I wish that everyone in the world were Catholics. It grieves me when Catholics leave My Church."

Fr. Doria: Now, let us pray for healing of the fear.

I, Fr. Doria, hear Jesus telling me this about the 2 examples: Out of the scandals I am raising up a Church of many pure, holy priests. Even though it is only just when lay people protest sexual sins of priests and cover-ups, I don't want them to be consumed with fear. Cling to the priests you trust, but also pray for repentance and conversion of the ones who have fallen.

About the Choir Director, I hear Jesus recommending that he have a long conversation with the new priest about the values he sees in what he has done for the parish. He could consider agreeing to having a Latin Gregorian Chant Mass once a month to start and that he would be willing to look into Chant.

Now try to see what Jesus is telling you about your fears in your own example.

I, Ronda, heard Jesus telling me that He has inspired me to love the Church and its truths, but that He also wants me to learn about other religions, not only to evangelize but also to appreciate what is good in their example. I could learn how to pray in greater contemplative silence to Him by putting aside more of my concerns, as Hindus and Zen masters do.

Fr. Doria: Many of you are tired. Some of you want to go to

Confession. This forgiveness prayer will be short.

Jesus, You taught us to forgive 77x7 times and to forgive our enemies. Please give each of us a spirit of forgiveness for each of the persons we have been remembering tonight. Amen.

I was too tired to go to Confession, but I was moved when Jim Marley came over to the table I was sitting at and gave me a silent hug.

As I was falling asleep, I thought humorously: a widower who had a good marriage to a nurturing motherly woman didn't necessarily want as a second wife a woman philosopher debater!!!

3.

DAY II

Liturgy – Communal vs. Transcendent

Catholic Church – One of Many Good Churches vs. One True Church

MORNING SESSION:

After breakfast the next morning, Fr. Doria gave an introductory talk to the participants about the morning theme.

He began with these remarks about the topics of the first day:

Fr. Doria: I have been giving a lot of thought to the question of anger. Several of you have challenged me along these lines: "There are plenty of people who dissent from Church teachings or are militantly loyal to them, but who are not angry. Maybe you need more categories in your Spectrum?"

Here is my experience. Those who are adherents of sides in most of these divisive issues, but are not angry, are still divisive just the same. For example, if a Catholic priest or professor calmly states that he/she thinks there ought to be same-sex marriages, this will divide him or her from those who absolutely don't think so, even if neither of the two interlocutors gets angry.

Or if a priest or professor starts talking about the glories of the Latin Tridentine Mass, those who dislike it, without becoming angry, may avoid that priest or that professor's courses from then on. Anger is not always hot. Cold anger is often expressed, not by yelling, but by withdrawal.

Now those of an angry temperament, also called cholerics, mostly will be much more angry than laid-back phlegmatics. But even usually laid-back Catholics can become extremely angry about particular issues.

However, if you hate not just the sin, but also the sinner, becoming less angry because of our dialogues and healing sessions will get you less years in purgatory!

(Laughter)

Our first topic for dialogue today is Liturgy. I have made up the terms Communal vs. Transcendent to avoid the usual Latin vs. Vernacular just to get you to think outside the box. Another way some put the division is horizontal vs. vertical.

Now, you don't have to be rocket scientists to realize that I, your host, try to blend the two poles. I believe Holy Mass should be warmly communal but also reverently transcendent.

So, does that make everyone happy who comes to our Masses at St. Athanasius?

Not really! Some tell me that if I was a true magisterial Catholic, I would be having the Tridentine Latin Mass here all the time. Others wish the music were less contemporary, with more of the old familiar traditional English hymns. Others, especially charismatics, want the gesture of peace to go on for 15 minutes with every participant shaking the hands of every other throughout the whole chapel!

Many Militant #4's, and all #5's, think that the whole problem is that so many Catholics no longer believe in the Real Presence of Christ in the Eucharist, thinking it is really just a symbol. They usually think that lack of belief in this mystery is because we no longer kneel at the altar to receive Holy Communion and the option to receive in the hand has led to less of a feeling of the sacredness of the Host.

Radical #1's think that having women priests would make the liturgy less patriarchal. Many post-Vatican II evolving Catholics, #2's, think the change to the vernacular and the elimination of the altar rails is precisely what Jesus wants. Less patriarchal because the priest isn't separated so much from the people as in the old liturgy or speaking in a language we don't understand. At the Last Supper, the language was probably Aramaic and the reception of the Eucharist was at a dining table.

I am sure you will have your own examples of divisions in the Church on liturgy.

Here are your questions for dialoguing with the same group you talked to yesterday for these more formal sessions:

> Did you ever regularly attend Masses in Latin before Vatican II? What did you like about them, or what did you not like?

> What do you like about the Masses you usually attend in your parish or Catholic institution now? What do you wish could be different?

> Again, don't interrupt or respond until each person has had his/her say.

When James and I settled down at our table with our coffee and snacks, I began saying with a laugh:

Here is where we don't fit easily into your #2 on the Spectrum or me with my #4, because I remember the one time I visited you at your home it was a Gregorian Chant convent you took me to for Sunday Mass.

James (smiling): Yes, I still go to that convent. I like the continuity with the old Church of my childhood. I rather dislike the contemporary hymns in most parishes – they are musically inferior.

Ronda: I'm an extremist on liturgy. I like best either charismatic

Masses with gospel type songs or high Latin Masses. One way I like to explain it is this – the Traditional Mass appeals to the soul. The contemporary Mass appeals to the psyche (as in how you come in feeling low, and then sing "Here I am, Lord" and you feel better). The charismatic Mass appeals to the gut (the passionate desire to be saved).

James: I am afraid emotion in religion has almost replaced the spiritual. Shouldn't the liturgy, precisely, elevate us into the world of the soul?

Ronda: Yes, but how can the Church claim to be a community when most of the parishioners don't even know each other's names, no less have deigned to even touch each other's hands?

Or, how about bad memories so many Catholics before Vatican II had of priests and sisters who were cruelly punishing? When I first taught Philosophy of God, one student answered the question "Who is God?" with the answer: "The one who can zap you out of existence."

James: I find some of those accounts of cruel priests and sisters to be exaggerated. They are always told as if the children were only mildly mischievous, whereas, in reality, many of them were punished for cruel or totally disruptive things they were doing.

I find that the key underlying problem about liturgy is that most Catholics walk into Church their minds still on their problems in family or work. Then they chat with friends until the Liturgy begins. I preferred when the people were taught to come early and become what we called "recollected," in contemporary language, deeply centered in Christ.

Ronda: That's certainly true. A priest who taught at St. Paul's in the theology department got me to wonder whether it wouldn't be better to have the weekend Mass as reverent as possible. A Praise and Worship service once a week would provide the opportunity for themes of loud praise and the exercise of the charismatic gifts of the Spirit.

James: Are you still involved with such prayer groups, Ronda? I heard the movement dwindled here in the United States.

Ronda: Yes, after years of thinking I belonged with lay groups such as Benedictine Oblates, or Franciscans, or Dominicans, I realized that my spirituality is essential charismatic. I go to a small parish prayer group every week.

James: Oh, we haven't talked yet about liturgical dance? Your twin sister, Carla De Sola, was a pioneer in that. I often saw her leading dancers at Masses here at St. Athanasius and at conferences.

Whenever I pray Psalm 149 "Let us praise the Lord with festive dance..." I think of her.

Ronda: Yes, she still has a company, now on the West Coast, called Omega West. Now there's a divisive matter. The U.S. Bishops banned dance at Mass many decades ago, but then in the document on liturgy from the Vatican it was left it up to the Bishop, and even John Paul II used to join in sacred dance with the parishioners when visiting Africa.

James: I love the way Carla dances and those in her company, but not always the liturgical dance of others who are less graceful.

Ronda: A huge issue that #4's and 5's bring up, is the distraction, especially for men, in seeing female bodies in motion during Mass where they want to concentrate on the spiritual. Others, however, think that the beauty of dance helps Mass-goers to avoid getting into a sort of numb, bored state of mind. It is more holistic.

James: The Eucharist itself is so holistic and incarnational. In other religious traditions the whole effort is to detach from everything physical. But in our Eucharist, we experience how Christ wants to enter into matter, right into our bodies.

Ronda: Yes! When I teach groups about spirituality, I like to encourage daily Mass for those who can go without difficulty. They seem to like this almost dance image I have: "If Jesus wants to leap down from heaven through the hands of the priest to enter your body, shouldn't you be there to receive Him?"

James smiled. "I like the imagery you use in your books, Ronda."

THE MASS:

During the homily Fr. Doria surprised some of us oldies with this story: I was giving a retreat for priests. I asked them to write on a piece of paper without their name on it what was their greatest joy as a priest. Ninety percent of them wrote: Celebrating the Eucharist.

LUNCH:

Fr. Doria: Let me remind you again not to sit at the same table with your morning sharing group and to spend part of the time telling others about incidents in the Church in general that helped you feel less divided from those in other categories in the Spectrum.

A younger theology professor strong on social justice issues told us about a militantly orthodox priest in his parish. This priest urged the people to go to confession for their sexual sins at least once a month in his homilies. But, at the same time, he personally led after-school programs for all the poor gang kids in his parish area. This kept this professor from thinking wrongly that all militantly orthodox priests on morality don't care about the poor.

I, Ronda, told about how moved I am when I see that someone I would rate as a #2 does something totally surprising. A Bishop I thought of as dissenter, when he used to visit the college where I taught, would walk around the quad saying the rosary on large beads. He also surprised me by coming to the first Operation Rescue pro-life protest before we arrived and telling the police that "If you harm any of these peaceful protestors you will go to hell!"

A philosophy professor told about how surprised she was to meet a layman who was joining an order of same-sex attraction men who would be promoting the Latin Mass! Now, of course, this would not be a possibility for the usual groups of Latin Mass proponents, but it shows how many unexpected things are going on in our Church right now.

Someone read an article claiming that some charismatics are moving toward the Latin Mass!

ADORATION:

In spite of a good nap, I came to Adoration in the chapel feeling tired and discouraged. So many divisions, so much anger.

"Jesus, help me. Why are You allowing all this mess in Your Church?"

It was consoling that Jesus seemed to tell me: I suffer with these divisions. Still, I have such joy in my good priest sons and consecrated religious and in faithful laity, such as you. When you feel sad, bury yourself in My heart.

AFTERNOON SESSION:

Fr. Doria: My friends, you know I don't have a Ph.D. in theology like many of you. So, instead of presenting a disquisition, I will simply tell you the way I see it.

My favorite image comes from John Paul II where he described the light of Christ in the Catholic Church being like the pinnacle of a triangle with rays extending downward. The idea was that other religions participate in the light in different ways.

Some would interpret such an image to mean that it doesn't matter what Christian Church or what religion you belong to as long as you follow the light you see.

That might be the perspective of some religious anthropologists, but it doesn't jibe with so many statements of Jesus about going forth to "baptize all nations 'In the Name of the Father, the Son, and the Holy Spirit.'" Or, as one of you Ph.D.'s once said about evangelization: "How could you know Jesus and not want everyone to know Him?"

We want to eschew a kind of indifferentism that was already gaining ground in the beginning of the 20th century.

On the other hand, no matter what the problems of ecumenical and inter-faith dialogue, few of us would want to go back to time where many Catholics only saw the errors in other religions and never acknowledged any truths at all in them.

So, here is your question for your afternoon small group sharings:

    Why are you still a Catholic?

Ronda: I don't think Fr. Doria has them, but I recently edited a whole series of booklets with that title: *Why I am Still a Catholic.* My purpose was to reach the many doubters of today's Church, often due to the scandals – but often the scandals are only the last straw of uneasiness sometimes over decades about many things.

James: It may seem simplistic but I am still a Catholic for the reason that I love the Church. I love her sacraments, I love her buildings, her art, her music, and especially her saintly mystics.

Ronda: Well put. A +, James. When I hear people saying they are leaving the Church over the scandals I say, "There was a scandalous football coach. I didn't notice anyone dropping watching football because of it!"

Just the same, you don't identify with Moderates or Militant Magisterial Catholics. How come?

James: I suppose because of the influence of Teilhard de Chardin, the great Jesuit archaeologist theologian who taught us to think in terms of evolution of the Church and the world. Moderates seem to me to lack passion. But Militants, even you, my dear old friend, seem to me to be so defensive as to lack openness to evolving truths.

Ronda: (smiling) Hmmmm! I actually read almost all of Teilhard de Chardin in graduate school. He was all the rage when I was studying here in the 60's. I came to think this way about his optimism. At the end of World War II, there was such relief, it opened some thinkers to want to believe that a new great world order would evolve. The Christian form of this optimism of Teilhard was to think we were moving from the Alpha to the Omega through the evolution of world history.

From a psychological standpoint I sometimes think that sanguines (optimists) go for this kind of false hope. Melancholics (pessimists), never! But since we should all be realists instead of optimists or pessimists, the 20th century where millions were killed by Soviet and Chinese Communists and 60 million innocent babies were aborted hardly looks like the ascent of mankind to an evolved fullness of justice!!!!

James: What of progress? Economic development of the world, sensitivity to ecological issues, greater equality of woman with men?

Ronda: Let's leave those topics to other days of this week. I wanted to tell you about how I have overcome doubts about the Church.

James: Go ahead. We have so much more time for these sessions it only being us, two, at this table.

Ronda: When I get doubts about the Church, I review in my mind all the reasons I became a Catholic so many years ago:

-   Philosophical proofs for the existence of God, and nowadays in addition the writings of scientists who insist science shows the existence of God.
-   Proofs for the divinity of Christ – like those of C.S. Lewis where there is no way He could just be a good person, or even a prophet given what His words meant in context of Judaism. As

well, I like to say that the *Passion of the Christ* movie proves the Resurrection, because how would the disciples ever have opened themselves up to such torture as it really was, if they hadn't seen the Resurrection.

- Proofs that Jesus wanted to form a Church. There is nothing in the New Testament that would ever give you the impression that He wanted single individuals to simply respond to Him and have nothing to do with other Christians!

- What about Protestant Churches? No way does private interpretation lead to stability of Church bodies – instead we have 40,000 Christian Churches from people deciding what Christ's truth is without a magisterial authority.

- Slowly learning in graduate school why the Church teaches that certain actions are intrinsically evil – not simply man-made rules.

- Seeing how saints of the past not only survived division but helped grow the Church for new generations out of the ashes of sinful patterns and false theories.

James: I would go along with all that you say, except that I don't think all of those points preclude growth throughout the centuries. Let's take something like slavery. In the time of the Old and New Testaments it was accepted. It took centuries before it was realized that slavery was incompatible with the free nature of human persons and could never be justified. Couldn't the same type of evolution occur in other areas of Catholic ethics?

Ronda: Aha! I happen to have researched that area for teaching ethics. I always insist on the difference between development of a teaching and contradiction, following the famous book of St. Cardinal Newman: *The Development of Catholic Doctrine.*

Briefly, slavery in the time of the Old and New Testament was the only alternative to killing the enemy when an army was victorious. It was more like indentured servitude. And slaves were not usually treated at all the way they were in the Americas in our early history.

When the slave trade began it was roundly denounced by the Magisterium of the Church, even though buying slaves already living in a country, with a view to using them as laborers, was not considered to be intrinsically evil. So, it was a development rather than a contradiction to insist that any kind of slave-like ownership of the labor of another human being is wrong.

Or, in the case of considering taking interest on a loan to be intrinsically wrong, but later allowing it, there was a change in society when, through banking, giving loans at interest became a help to the poorer citizens. So, it is argued, it is still intrinsically wrong to charge exorbitant interest on a loan. But giving loans and having them paid back with interest is a development rather than a contradiction.

James: Splitting hairs, perhaps? Why not say that changing historical conditions can alter moral teaching? So, when young people married at age 13 and 15 at puberty it was easier to be chaste until marriage, whereas now it is much harder, at the peak of sexual energy, to wait for some 10 years to marry. And, so, a couple lacking the finances to marry while in college could have sex while engaged, no?

Ronda (raising her voice) Yeah, sure, and meanwhile using contraceptives which at least half the time destroy the already formed embryo in the womb or aborting the baby if they conceive in spite of contraceptives???

(I was getting very angry.)

James: Those topics will come up again tomorrow. Meanwhile, it's almost dinner-time.

DINNER:

Fr. Doria: That was a pretty heavy topic. How about relaxing at dinner and talking about something totally different such as what your all-time favorite movies or novels are?

Due to the age differences between us, choices at this dinner ranged all the way from *Gone with the Wind*, and the *Sound of Music*, and, mine, *Fiddler on the Roof*, to *Hero* and *Matrix*.

HEALING SESSION:

I came to the healing session exhausted from the argument in the afternoon with James. I was eager to see what Fr. Doria could say to help me have more hope.

Fr. Doria: Let me remind you that we have Confession at 8 P.M.

(I wondered if I should confess getting so angry at James about sex outside of marriage.)

Fr. Doria began with a prayer of thanksgiving for our Liturgy and for our Church itself, host of Holy Mass:

Dear God, we thank you for sending Your Son to create a way of worship so mystical and beautiful as is this memorial of His Crucifixion and Resurrection. We thank you for all the priests throughout the centuries who have given their lives to make the Eucharist possible for us.

We thank you that throughout the centuries Your Holy Spirit has triumphed over so many divisions and we pray that, indeed, one day we all may be one in faith.

Now I ask each one of you here present to enter into this thanksgiving from the depth of your heart during 10 minutes of silence.

During that silent time, I, Ronda, prayed, "Oh, my Jesus, let me never take for granted our sacred liturgy and Your Church with all its holy sacraments."

Fr. Doria then continued: For some of you the authority of the Magisterium of the Church has become controversial. You may associate different 20-21st Century Popes with teachings you disagree with. You may believe that those in your spectrum of the Church are championing the teachings of the future Church that Jesus wants to replace some antiquated teachings of the past. Or, you may think that the present Pope is trying to replace the true teachings with erroneous ones.

Here is my prayer for you if such is the case:

Jesus, my Lord, my Savior, beloved Friend and Teacher, please enlighten the minds, hearts, and souls of all here present that nothing contrary to the truth may hold us captive.

Even when we are convinced that we believe only what You have revealed in Scripture and through tradition, help us to speak that truth with love so that we may not stir up contradiction by our very manner of presenting it!

(Surely that last was a word for me, I thought ruefully.)

As I enunciate an examination of conscience I wrote for this group, consider anything that rings true as something to ponder for Confession this evening or in the future:

-   If there is any perennial teaching of the Church that I have doubted or rejected because I needed to rationalize about some sin or weakness in my own life, let me humbly admit to this origin of dissent.

- If there are teachings of others in the Spectrum that have truth in them that I glide over because I resent other beliefs of those Catholics, help me to ponder them to achieve greater balance.

- If I have been demeaning and ridiculing, in conversation with opponents of the truth, or in my own way of describing them to my allies, may I learn from the Holy Spirit, how to speak the truth in love.

At that point, Fr. Doria dimmed the lights reminding us that Confession would be available in 30 minutes.

I, Ronda, made a general confession of years and years of speaking the truth with anger vs. love.

4.

DAY III

Sexuality and Marriage: Ideals vs. Obligations

Universal Salvation vs. Purgatory, Hell, and Heaven

MORNING SESSION:

Fr. Doria (smiling):

Dear friends, I bet these topics are the ones you are most upset about no matter where you are on the Spectrum!

Now our morning topic spans a long list of controversial issues all the way from sexual abuse and rape, to masturbation, porn, pre-marital sex, same-sex attraction acted out and marriage of same-sex couples, extra-marital sex, contraception, divorce, and abortion.

I know many of you consider abortion to be primarily a social justice issue. Just the same it seems odd to me that people sometimes talk about unwanted babies as if they came about by magic, with some woman suddenly finding she is having a baby – as if she had done nothing that brought this about – which is only true in the case of rape, surely not the most frequent cause of unwanted babies!

Now some of you think that our Church's teachings need to evolve in some of these areas, and some believe the teachings are not only traditional but also eternally unchangeable.

One form of this division is where some professors and some priests claim that traditional moral teachings in the area of sexuality and marriage are ideals rather than strict obligations. So, for instance, one could say that never masturbating is an ideal, but since this form of release is so common among young males, it doesn't need to be confessed each time as a sin. I am told that in sex-education programs girls are also taught masturbation is healthy.

On a related formulation, about evolving doctrine, I don't find that anyone thinks rules should evolve when they agree with them! Can you imagine someone saying we have to let our traffic laws evolve in contemporary times so that good drivers can do 90 mph during rush hour!

On a timely topic, some think that only Spectrum #1's and #2's commit mortal sins in the sexual area. I like to point out that the scandals of a priest of one of the magisterial orders ever in the Church was one of the worst. His story also shows us that we cannot judge about scandals because we know and admire someone since it appears that even so gifted a judge of character as John Paul II didn't understand what this priest was covering!

I believe it is better when reading of scandals, unless we ourselves are personally involved as victims or judges, to pray for all in those situations, not only in a perfunctory way, but from the heart. "There but by the grace of God go I" is a better prayer than "Thank you, God, I am not like him or her!"

Here are some questions for your sharing times this morning:

1. What are some of the ways you have taught Catholic ethics in the area of sexuality and marriage that have been most effective?

2. As Ph.D.'s and Professors, how do you find that personalism helps you to explain the moral teachings of the Church in the area of sexuality and marriage?

As you see I have purposely made the questions for this morning session positive sounding. This is to give you a chance to share insights without leaping immediately into argument.

Again, allow each person at your table to speak without interrupting!

Once at our table again, the dialogue proceeded:

James (laughing): How about setting a volume control on your speech on these explosive topics?

Ronda (smiling): I better, or I'll have to make an hour Confession tonight for sarcasm and rage!

James: Let me begin. Raised in pre-Vatican II times by old-fashioned Southern Catholics, I learned the standard ways to understanding sexual ethics and marriage. No sex outside of marriage; no divorce except for such reasons as the spouse being a bigamist or concealing something huge such as being the type of homosexual who hates sex with anyone but same-sex partners.

At St. Athanasius, when studying for the Ph.D. in theology, moral theology had already become, let's say, nuanced. Yes, masturbation was wrong because it is solo sex outside of marriage, but that didn't mean that every young man had to follow the example of John XXIII, who wrote in his autobiography that he tied his hands together with a rope before he went to sleep!

Or, the idea was already floating about before Vatican II that whereas genital sex outside of marriage was wrong, everything up to that would not be sinful in the case of a couple who loved each other!!!

Ronda: (interrupting) Right! One of my best arguments about sex between engaged couples that I lay on my students is this: So, if breaking an engagement isn't a sin, then engagement isn't a full commitment the way marriage is. And then how can engagement fit the obligation that sex should only take place when the couple has married, thus building a nest for future babies!

James: Now, Ronda, remember Fr. Doria's rule? You're interrupting me!

Ronda: Sorry!

James: To avoid misunderstanding, it happens that my Catholic family background kept me chaste until marriage, which wasn't until I was twenty-eight, so I am not trying to rationalize the sins of my youth!

Ronda: I didn't know that. I'm impressed! I remember once asking a student of mine who was holding out for sex with her beloved until marriage, why they didn't get married right away. Her reply astounded me. "Oh, Dr. Chervin, we would hate to desecrate the noble sacrament of marriage by rushing into it just to be able to have sex!!"

James: I have never taught moral theology. I much prefer teaching spirituality. I believe that Catholics could better avoid the temptations of sin if they had a much deeper prayer life than most of them have.

Ronda: I have seen that in working with married couples on their spirituality. For example, marriage encounter has kept many couples from divorce. They begin to pray together every evening and converse instead of escaping into TV.

James: I am presently reading a book by a Benedictine monk recounting locutions from Jesus. He is told by Jesus that if priests spent an hour every day in adoration prayer, they would have so intimate a relationship to Him that they would not seek solace for loneliness in sinful liaisons.

Ronda: Yes, I think he is right….I love the way post-abortion healing counseling brings women who have had abortions into the forgiving heart of Jesus.

James: Let's look at the second question: As Ph.D.'s and Professors, how do you find personalism helps you to explain the moral teachings of the Church in the area of sexuality and marriage?

Ronda: Having studied for years with Dietrich Von Hildebrand who taught what would now be called a personalist ethics, I have a lot to say about that. It is because of the beauty of the sacrament of marriage, with the couple enfolded in the love of Jesus, that the deviations can better be seen as so tragic and destructive. I am told that nowadays people are expected to have sex with each other by the 3rd date! I mean, how different is it if the couple views their child as the reflection of their love for the unique preciousness of their spouse, than if they see the baby growing in the womb as simply the unwanted outcome of a brief love affair!

James: Even though sex outside of marriage is wrong, wouldn't it be better if couples who are just dating used contraceptives?

Ronda: Oh, good. You gave me an opening for my favorite teachings about this. Here is the simplest one:

People ask, if the couple doesn't want to have a child at a particular time, what difference does it make if they use contraceptives or natural family planning? (If you, the reader, don't happen to know about natural family planning, it's a method of tracking the part of the woman's menstrual cycle to see when she is fertile and then avoiding sexual intercourse at those times of the month.)

Here is my analogy. An uncle brings his nephew a beautiful bicycle for Christmas. The nephew is told to bring the bicycle to the basement because he can't ride it with snow on the ground. So, he postpones using the gift. That is like natural family planning – postponing using the gift of fertility. But suppose the nephew gets angry and grabs a hammer and breaks the bicycle. That is like destroying the fertile sperm or blocking the egg or flushing out with a pill the already formed embryo. It is rejecting God's gift of our fertile nature.

Now, here is another analogy. Before the Black is Beautiful movement, many blacks tried to look as white as possible by straightening their curly hair, whitening their faces, etc. Then, with the Black is Beautiful trend, Blacks started showing off their curly hair, wearing African motif clothing, etc.

Here's the analogy. A woman should not be thinking of her God-given fertile time as "my bad time." She should not be trying with contraceptives to be just like a man who can have sex without getting pregnant. She should be saying to any man, if you have sex with me when I am fertile, expect to become a father!

James: Those are fascinating analogies. I will ponder them. But what of the plight of people with genetically caused same-sex attraction who won't have biological children. Should they have no chance to seal their love for each other with physical affection?

Ronda: This idea of homosexuality as a fated biological trait has no scientific evidence. You should read the basic Catholic books by pioneers in the Courage movement such as Harvey and Nicolosi. Fr. Harvey started the Courage movement – it is like a 12 Step for same-sex attraction people who try to be chaste. Dr. Nicolosi, a practicing psych-therapist who specializes in counseling same-sex attraction people insists that anyone can become bi-sexual if they are willing to undergo in depth therapy!

Recently I was talking to an old friend of mine who is knowledgeable about the history of same-sex attraction. He asked me if I knew how many famous homosexuals, starting with the Greeks, also were married with children? He claims that the overwhelming majority are not men or women who cannot have sex with the opposite gender, but rather those who enjoy opposite sex encounters at the same time as same-sex, as an alternate type of pleasure!

Ronda: Oh, it happened that on my way to the cafeteria for breakfast, I ran into a former student of mine from St. Paul's who gave me a short paper she wrote about the personalist approach to homosexuality.

I rifled through my tote bag and found this and showed it to James:

"Sexuality is for the sacred union of two people for the main purpose of having children.

"True love of any kind is an intimacy between two souls, an emotional and spiritual connection. A true deep love doesn't have to be sexual. In fact, adding sexuality harms a relationship outside of marriage.

"Everyone is searching for love. No one can live without love, no matter how old or rich or accomplished.

"Anyone can (and many, many have) lived a full and joyful life without ever having sexual intimacy. Think of good moral priests and Sisters. It's a dangerous lie that your life has to be unfulfilled if you don't have romantic - sexual experiences.

"A woman is meant to love other women deeply, as a man is meant to love other men deeply. For many, homosexuality is this deep, beautiful desire to connect on a deep level with other people of the same sex. This desire is a godly desire. For who can understand you best other than someone who shares your most essential human feature - your maleness or femaleness.

"We are created for connection, for intimacy. Everyone is looking for friendship, a deep, strong, and yes, *eternal* connection. No one wants love to end, to die. Homosexuality distorts this wonderful God-given desire to love those who are most like us into something carnal.

"In fact, the Bible exquisitely shows the depth of love between two men: From 2 Samuel 1:2

I grieve for you, Jonathan my brother!

Most dear have you been to me;
More wondrous your love to me
than the love of women.

"One other factor that has led to the increase in homosexuality activity and many people's view that it is their right to be happy is the way the vast majority of heterosexuals live their lives. So, if a man and a woman don't wait to get married to have sex, why should the homosexual live without sex? But if the heterosexual regarded sexual activity as only permissible in the marital union and lived chaste lives until (and IF) they married, they would also set a good example to those with homosexual inclinations.... that it is possible to be chaste."

James: That is beautiful, Ronda. You can tell that former student of yours she needs to become a writer. I think that I was naïve about same-sex attraction when I was in graduate school, especially homosexuality among males. With no experience of it and not knowing anyone of that inclination growing up, I thought such relationships were like engaged or married couples - a tender embrace. I was horrified later on in life to read statistics about many homosexual males having 4 encounters a day with strangers in men's rooms!

At this point, Fr. Doria came in to lead us into the cafeteria for lunch.

Fr. Doria: Again I urge you to sit with others at different parts of the Spectrum and to talk at lunch about positive experiences that contradict stereo-types.

One younger woman who was close to Catholics of the #5 category, Traditionals, offered this unexpected anecdote:

"This friend of mine who only goes to Latin Masses told me they strictly forbid any girls or women to wear leggings to Church."

Ronda: "You mean tights, like dancers?"

She replied, "Ronda, you are behind the times. They are now called leggings, and they are those form-fitting pants that totally outline the bottoms of the wearers…anyhow, so I laughed and said I thought that was extreme! But, then a man who was with us at the coffee hour after Mass, exclaimed – "They're dead right. I experience terrible temptations of lust every time I see a girl or woman in one of those leggings!"

Another diner talked about how a Latin Mass priest I knew told me once that Traditionals confess the same sins as so-called Post-Vatican II Catholics.

A pro-life activist mentioned how consoling it was to him when Daniel Berrigan, the famous anti-war priest, marched in a Pro-Life rally.

Even though I knew it would be very emotional, I told my luncheon group about something unexpected after my son's suicide. Two of the priests at St. Paul's College whom I battled with the most about ethical issues involving sex and marriage were passing by the bridge off which my son had jumped to his death. They got out of their car and said a

Mass for him at the spot where they thought he must have landed!

MASS:

Fr. Doria included in his homily this story:

"I was con-celebrating a Sunday Mass with a priest friend from the seminary we both attended. He began his homily by asking the congregation: "Can you guess why I weep in the middle of the night?"

There was a profound silence.

"I weep for those of you who don't receive Holy Communion because you are married outside Church without an annulment of your first marriages that might have been possible."

He enumerated reasons for annulment that most of the people were unaware of and ended with this stunner:

"Do you know that if you're are older and living like brother and sister at this point, you can come to Confession for marrying outside the Church, and receive Holy Communion for the rest of your days together?"

A year later this priest told me his office was flooded with people coming back to Holy Communion. Others who were civilly married but receiving Holy Communion without ever dealing with the issue of their first Catholic marriages began the process of seeing if their first marriages were truly valid or could be annulled (that is declared by canon-lawyers as lacking some essential element of marriage, as in when one or the other is too mentally ill to sustain a healthy relationship, for instance in the case of battering the spouse).

Do you see how this approach of the priest was passionate and loving and far from the caricature of old-fashioned priests just rejecting people for not following the rules?

May all of us "speak the truth with love" in every encounter even with opponents!"

ADORATION:

As I sat quietly gazing at the Monstrance with the large Host I prayed:

"Most Sacred Heart of Jesus," purge my heart of anger. In whatever number of years remain of my life, let my thoughts and words be purified of sarcasm and one-upmanship."

AFTERNOON SESSION:

Fr. Doria: "Enter through the narrow gate." (Matthew7:13) I am happy all of you have stayed with this, no matter how tiring and often painful it is to delve into these topics.

Here are some typical remarks spanning our Spectrum on the subject of life after death:

"Most people go to Hell. That is what Mary says in her Apparitions."

"A loving God could never banish anyone to hell. We should hope that everyone in any religion or lack of religion gets a chance to repent of sin."

"At the moment of death, everyone sees Jesus. Those who are basically good in spite of defects will rush toward Him. Those who don't, are damning themselves."

"We cannot know who goes to which place, even whether it is a place vs. a state of soul. We shouldn't judge anyone; only encourage them in their good aspirations."

Here are your questions for the afternoon session:

> Do you think that everyone is saved? Where do you think most people go after death? How do you think about your own transition to eternal life?

Ronda: I'd like to start with the last question. I like to put it jokingly: I hope to get an A for effort even though I am such a failure at being holy. So, I think that if I don't make purgatory, very few will. I love purgatory because for me it means home free at last!

James: I love the famous statement of Jung. Asked whether he believed in God, he replied. "I don't believe in God. I know God." Jesus has the key to the secret of my soul. I believe he will bring me through death into the realm He has readied for me by His union with me in prayer now.

Ronda: On the other questions, I prefer the alleged revelation of Mary at the Apparitions at Medjugorje – that most people go to purgatory. Given that so many people over the centuries since Adam didn't even know of God the Father, no less God the Son, I think it is judgmental to think that because they have sinned so many would go to hell. I prefer to think the way C.S. Lewis put it, that Fr. Doria quoted, that at death everyone sees Jesus, and if they love goodness they rush toward Him even if they didn't know Him before.

Now, I don't remember Lewis talking about purgatory, but I theorize that we can't enter into heavenly bliss until there is nothing but love in our hearts. In purgatory, in some mysterious way, we are purged of those pockets of non-forgiveness, resentment or trustlessness that block the triumph of Love.

James: I find the concept of God punishing people in hell seems too much like a projection of a father punishing a bad child. I prefer to imagine how His love seen by them at the time of death will itself purge them of the way they ran toward sin in despair of real love.

Ronda: I see what you mean, but still…re-reading the Gospel of St. Matthew recently, it is full of Jesus threatening with punishment in hell.

When #1's, #2's and #3's say things like God loves you all and never punishes, doesn't that leave the impression that no one needs Confession? And if, at every funeral, the consoling rhetoric gives the impression that all are going right to heaven, doesn't that convey an idea that no one needs Confession? And why have Masses for the souls of the dead deemed to be in purgatory if everyone goes straight to heaven?

James: Responding to your reading of the Gospel of St. Matthew, couldn't the threats of Jesus be like the way an angered father or mother might use threats to convince a child not to do something dangerous and destructive? Take a parental threat, "If you throw the food you don't like on the floor, you will never eat another meal in this house!" It doesn't really mean not that they will ever banish their child, but rather something like, "Please be grateful for the food we serve?"

Ronda: The Catechism holds that we cannot think that no one goes to hell since Jesus mentions it so often. Just the same we can't put them there since we are not the judge.

Sometimes I think the divide here on this issue of universal salvation vs. hell, or usually purgatory going toward heaven, is really a matter of temperament. Sanguines (optimists) always want to focus on the triumph of the good. Melancholics (pessimists) grieving for all the evil in themselves and in others want fear of punishment to lead to repentance and reform!

James: Don't we need to be realistic rather than optimistic or pessimistic? Wouldn't that lead not to insisting on justice in the final judgment, but rather on mercy? We could admit to all the evil in us and others so that we could never demand that we are entitled on heavenly bliss. Yet, at the same time trust in His mercy, hoping that all will be saved?

Ronda: But those who teach universal salvation rarely talk about the need for repentance! Think of the usual length of Confessional lines on Saturday afternoons before Vatican II, and now!

DINNER:

Fr. Doria told us to use our dinner time for informal conversation to tell about some 20th Century holy person each of us admires.

Ronda discusses saintly heroes at the dinner table with other attendees.

At my table of four, these were the persons described:

Dorothy Day, John Paul II, Oscar Romero, Mother Teresa of Calcutta.

HEALING SESSION:

Fr. Doria: Consider some slangy expressions:

"Go to hell!"
"Damn it!"
"You're an 'f_____ing' s.o.b."

Of course, no Ph.D. in Catholic philosophy or theology ever uses such expressions!
(Laughter)

I won't take a poll!

(Laughter)

I am being humorous to make a serious point. Namely, often times we focus on the most extreme sins of others in the category of sex and marriage, with the unconscious intention of minimizing our own!

Here is a chance to come clean! Suppose you spend the next half hour remembering any of your own sins in these areas, especially ones that haunt you!

One way to do this is to think of those in your whole lifetime you would feel embarrassed meeting in purgatory some day!

Suppose, not just concerning these areas of sin, but all of them, that purgatory consisted of experiencing all the pain you ever caused others during your whole lifetime. And suppose release from purgatory to heaven came when the forgiveness of others for those sins of yours, opened your heart to also forgive those who sinned against you?

The priests will be waiting for you in the Confessional at 8 PM.

By the way, those of you who love Mary and pray the rosary every day, have probably noticed that I didn't schedule a rosary even though it is my favorite prayer besides the Mass itself. This is because the rosary itself has become a source of division. Not in itself, because Catholics in all the divisions of the Spectrum pray it, but because of the Fatima prayer so many say at the end of each decade that includes the words "save us from the fires of hell." I find that most of those for whom hell is only a symbol find those words repugnant. However, I was happy to see some of you praying the rosary silently during your Adoration time.

Ronda: Even though I had been to confession the evening before, I found plenty to bring this night.

5.

DAY IV

Scriptures in Context vs. Scriptures as Normative

Roles: Feminism vs. Complementarity

MORNING SESSION

Fr. Doria: I am so happy to see all of you this week. I am praying that good insights are making it worth your while. And, especially, that the Holy Spirit may be teaching us in ways we may not have expected.

Today's morning topic, as all you who are theologians, surely know, is as controversial as any of the others

On this topic, the extremes of the divisions among all Christians about Scripture as literal or not. Some are absolute fundamentalist literalists, especially the Scripture passages which they take to define the type of Christianity they believe is the best. An example would be "Call no man father" (Matthew 23:9), used by some Christian groups to prove that Catholics are disobedient to Jesus since we call our priests Father. Yet, St. Paul calls himself a father of the faithful (1 Cor. 4) and few fundamentalist literalists refuse to call their birth or adopted fathers by the name "Father." Sayings of Jesus, such as call no man "Father," were not meant to be rules of speech, as if Jesus never called Joseph, Father. Rather, He was teaching us about the primacy of the Fatherhood of God.

And others would be in the extreme about the interpretation of Scripture by teaching that everything is myth and that this is good. Now in scholarly circles the word "myth" doesn't mean something false as it does in ordinary language. It means that what is thought to be a literal, historical idea is really something symbolic. An extreme example would be those who teach that the accounts of the Resurrection are not about a physical resurrection but, instead, our Christian myths about the experience of the rebirth of the soul when it reaches deeper levels of union with God. But, I would say that if even the Resurrection is a "myth" in the sense not of "false" but of "only symbolic," then Christianity ceases to be a historical religion and becomes simply one among many symbolic systems!

Now does that mean that if we ever look into the context of a Scriptural text we are violating its literal meaning or that we are in danger of understanding it only as a symbol?

Hardly. I am happy to read scholars who explain the context of Jesus condemning the guest at the wedding who wasn't wearing a wedding garment (Matthew 22:11-12). It is explained that at weddings of that time all the guests received the garment on entering the banquet hall – so that guest would have taken it off!

I was happy to hear once that when Jesus tells the woman who was not Jewish that she is like a dog who doesn't get the food the children, (Matthew 15:26) that this was a known form of banter at that time. The first speaker says something outrageous to call out a humorous response, such as the woman gives about the dogs at the table eating the scraps.

I am happy to read that the word for brothers at the time of Jesus included cousins, which explains why mention is made of the brothers of Jesus in several places, while we Catholics and some other Christians believe He was an only child.

On the other hand, I am not happy when some Scripture scholars seem to use context to eviscerate the meaning, as in claiming that Jesus only uses the word Father about the first person of the Trinity because his culture was patriarchal!

Here is your question for this morning's group sessions:

In what ways does context help you to understand Scripture? In what ways do you think it is normative – that is, has a meaning that transcends cultures and eras and is true for all Christians for all times?

AT THE TABLE:

Ronda: I have never studied hermeneutics, but you have James. Give me enough of a definition of terms so I can express myself more clearly about it.

James: Hermeneutics is the interpretation of texts, mostly Biblical ones. In Catholic theology, we distinguish four senses that can be found in Scriptures:

> The Literal – but, still, that includes something of the historical context, such as what the word "brother" meant in the languages of the New Testament.

> The Moral – such as how Moses was commanded by God to break the stones on which the Commandments were written to punish the people for their idolatry.

> The Allegorical – as in something like Noah's ark is a type of the Church in the New Testament.

> The Anagogical – a mystical interpretation such as in the analysis of numbers in the Bible in the Kabbalah.

Ronda: I find that most Catholic parishioners get confused by this. They don't always see clearly which passages in the New Testament are literal and which are more allegorical. So, I like to refer to Flannery O'Connor's unusual way to refute the literal fundamentalism of many of the Protestant Churches in the South where she lived. She wrote a famous short story about a man who is convinced that since he has so much lust he must literally pluck out his eye!!!

(James laughs)

On the other hand, I have never met any Catholics except strong, strong, Franciscan friars, who literally only have one piece of clothing as Jesus claims his disciples should do with.

James: Of course, much harder to understand is in what way the Real Presence of Jesus in the Eucharist is not merely symbolic in the allegorical sense, but clearly doesn't mean literal cannibalism as the Romans sometimes denounced the early Christians for practicing!

Ronda: Right. But, then, is it because they think of the Eucharist as *merely* symbolic that so few Catholics believe in the famous Eucharistic Miracles such as Lanciano, Orvieto, Poland, Betania, and recently in Buenos Aires, Argentina. In the last case, a host that had been discarded by a recipient and found on the floor showed itself to be real blood that scientists, including an atheist, identified as from the same person as that of centuries old Lanciano miracle.

James: I do not think of the Eucharist as "merely" symbolic, but rather as the apex of how God is omnipresent in everything. But, to diverge a moment. I wanted to bring up something that has been bothering me from the start of this seminar, Ronda. Even though Fr. Doria was careful to not limit the Spectrum he devised to liberals and conservatives, the way the topics are set up reminds me of the opening I sometimes use in my Contemporary Theology classes:

"I fear sometimes that conservatives, not just liberals, are like the

Pharisees - Catholics, but with a strong, unloving determination to be right; whereas the Camino Real of Christ is a chivalric way, romantic, full of fire and passion, riding on the pure, high-spirited horses of the self with their glad, high-stepping knees and flaring nostrils, and us with jingling spurs and the cry, "Mon joie!" – the battle cry of Roland and Oliver. Our Church is the Church of Passion." (John E. Senior)

Or, to put it another way, I don't approach God or the Church in terms of divisions about various topics, but rather in a mystical way. I want to dwell in God in such a way that I am more and more living on earth out of His Presence to His creation. So, if some line in Scripture stands out for me, it is not in terms of proof-texting but more as something to draw me deeper into the heart of God.

Ronda: Well, of course, that's beautiful. I define a mystic as one who experiences the supernatural in a heightened way vs. only by faith. And in that sense, I am also a mystic. But, but, but...going back to your point about the Eucharist being symbolic in a good way as the apex of His omnipresence...surely the presence of Jesus in the Eucharist is so supernatural and not the same kind of ontological presence God has in, say, a mosquito! And if this distinction is not made, then you have the teens of Post Vatican II often preferring God's presence at the beach to His presence in the Mass!

And, but, but, but...seeing Scripture as normative has really huge existential ethical consequences. Yes, but....suppose someone thinks contraception is never admonished in Scripture and just comes out of some medieval anti-sex tradition, not knowing that the word magic was forbidden and included the means of contraception in those days. So, because they don't know the actual meanings of words in Scripture, they can more easily think it is okay to use the pill because 'I felt so good when I used the it for the first time, to be able to have sex without worrying about babies.'

James: It is in Scripture?

Ronda: Not the pill in those times, but it came under the name of "magic" for it was considered magic that someone could stick different herbs in their wombs that would prevent the sperm from entering. And that was forbidden.

Now, take pre-marital sex – it was called fornication. So, when it is not translated, some people think adultery is forbidden but that sex outside of marriage for singles isn't!!

James: I always thought that since I loved God, I should love the body He created and not violate its nature.

LUNCH:

During lunch, the seminar participants talked about insights into Scriptures that came from historical exegesis.

"I learned a lot when I understood why there were Jewish people all over the Roman Empire, and that explains why legends such as that Mary lived in the company of St. John in Ephesus could have been true, or that Mary Magdalene eventually live in France as a hermitess."

"I used to wonder about the response of Mary to the Angel 'How can this be since I know not man?' After all, if you are engaged and expect soon to be married you would be expecting to have a child. Then I learned about how Mary and Joseph were probably part of the Essene sect that encouraged some married people to live in celibacy."

"Seeing what crucifixion was actually really like, as Mel Gibson researched it for the movie *The Passion*, gave me this insight. The crucifixion is, in a way, the proof of the resurrection because what disciples who knew what it was really like would risk such a thing unless they had seen Jesus resurrected?"

ADORATION:

Usually, I am pretty distracted during silent Adoration of the Blessed Sacrament, but today I was too tired from the seminar to indulge in analytic thinking about projects or family problems. Instead, I opened to Him from the bottom of my heart, asking:

"Jesus, we need you so much in the Church. You see how divided we are and what doubts assail us. Show us what You want of each of us in these troubled times."

I felt a fiery yearning in my heart. Then, after a while, Jesus seemed to say to me: "I am the Lord of My Church. The hope and healings must come not from your debates but from My heart. Do not speculate too much. Await My graces."

AFTERNOON SESSION:

Fr. Doria: "Creator God, You chose to make us to be some males, some females. You gifted us with positive masculine and positive feminine traits. After the Fall, though, we also have many negative traits. Jesus and Mary and Joseph manifested all positive traits. They also surprised many by traits not always associated with their biological type. Jesus compared himself to a mother-hen, and Mary uttered phrases about God casting down the mighty you would not expect of a housewife! Help us as we explore our viewpoints about roles of men and women to avoid limiting stereotypes but also to avoid culturally limited trends as well."

Here are 3 theories about women's and men's roles in society and Church prevalent in the past and still competing for attention in our times. (I am only presenting very simple definitions – there are sub-types within these categories who disagree on important points at issue today in the world and in the Church.)

Complementarity: The theory that God created men and women to be different and these differences lead to differing roles. Examples: Women, having bodies capable of bearing and feeding babies, are suited to be mothers. Men, with stronger bodies, are more suited for strenuous physical activities such as hunting or construction. Men with a wider range of knowledge of the world around them are better as leaders and managers. Women, closer to the heart, are better at more personal activities such as nursing. These differences make them a good team.

Feminism: The theory that roles for the sexes were constructed in society for the benefit of men. Patriarchy leads to exploitation of women and should be overthrown. All roles should be open to everyone regardless of each one's sex. No discrimination should be accepted. Such roles include the priesthood.

Wholeness: All women have a masculine side and all men a feminine side. No traits are only for one sex and not another. It is limiting to have a division of roles. A good man needs to have many characteristics usually seen as feminine such as being nurturing and compassionate. A good woman needs to be strong and intelligent.

Here are your questions:

1. How did you think of the roles of men and women in society and in the Church before becoming a graduate student of philosophy or theology?

2. Did any stereotypes in the culture or the Church impact your hopes and dreams?

3. What in your professional studies in this area do you consider to be most significant?

Ronda: James, I am sure I must have given you the book I wrote entitled *Feminine, Free, & Faithful*, about just these topics, but I don't remember what you thought about it.

James: Since we are around the same age, my friend, you will understand that I only have a vague idea about that book of yours. I remember that I found it stimulating. I like to relate to the people I know as individuals rather than as exemplifications of theories. As a male child growing up in the South, I remember liking the way even strong men had soft voices and even soft women could be powerful when it came to decisions in the family.

Ronda: In my case, I was brought up to be what would now be called feminist, though the term didn't exist then. I was always a strong talker. But I disliked that my mother wore slacks before they became popular. She looked strange among other mothers of school children who wore pretty dresses. My heroines were my mother's favorite actress, Katherine Hepburn, who was smart, but also Scarlett O'Hara, the seductress.

James: I was certainly brought up to think that I could succeed at any masculine role I chose. And, I will admit, I was surprised to find there were women philosophy and theology graduate students, expecting them instead to be in elementary education or nursing or secretarial work.

Ronda: I was uncertain about what I wanted to do professionally. Still in the late 1950's I was not surprised when the guidance counselor at my college thought that no woman could be happy as a philosophy professor and that I should look into something more satisfying such as cooking!

James: I don't think it was until way after Vatican II that we ever even talked about women as possible priests. After all, the Sisters were leaders as school principals and hospital administrators, and the women saints were such powerful personalities that they seemed dominant over many of the priests in their communities. When I teach about the doctors of the Church, I love to recount how a priest of the Inquisition, after examining St. Teresa of Avila, remarked not only that she was orthodox, but also that she was "a strong man!"

Ronda: I liked to challenge my students by pointing out that it was after Vatican II, when many Churches took out the statues of the saints (half of whom were women) and the huge pictures of Mary, Mother of God, that Catholics started talking about how masculine the Church was.

James: (laughing) But, Ronda, just the same, you can't think that having an all-male priesthood doesn't lead to such negatives as clericalism, paternalism, and women thinking they have little say in broader Church directives.

Ronda: Surprisingly, for a woman professor, perhaps, I like having strong men in authority. It makes me feel secure. Surveys show that not only most men, but also most women, prefer male speakers and professors to women in those roles.

I think there is a contradiction built into the very word "feminism." You would think it meant love of the feminine, but instead it means trying to be like men, and not only in traditionally positive male traits such as strength and leadership but also by becoming negatively masculine, as in ruthless and dominating. I mean, what could be more ruthless than having your own baby killed by mostly male doctors in order to proceed with your own career!

James: I would agree with most of what you say, Ronda, but you seem to be leaving out a lot. Certainly, women have been treated brutally all the way from wife-beating to rape. Certainly, they have been exploited for low wages throughout the whole world. And I doubt if women priests would be as prone to scandalous exploitation of minors as some male priests have been.

Ronda: If feminism means fighting oppressive actions of men with negative masculine traits, that part of it is good. John Paul II promoted what he called Christian feminism. But he still insisted that Jesus being the Son of God could not be represented by female priests. I like to ask doubters about this whether you would have a famous male actor play the role of Mary in a Nativity play in your parish?

DINNER:

Fr. Doria suggested that we relax at dinner by telling anecdotes about favorite Catholic women and men we had known well. It was refreshing.

When I had my turn, I talked about a few dear people who combine positive traits of both sexes, leading to a lot of wholeness. My godfather was a German philosophy professor, Balduin Schwarz, teaching in the US, who was extremely mild of temperament but strong as can be in fidelity to the Church and to all those he directed spiritually. A French friend of mine, also living in the US, is extremely good at efficient prudent management of vast real estate holdings but becomes absolutely compassionate in a motherly way whenever anyone is in pain. She is a wonderful counselor of pregnant women who come for help at her pro-life maternity outreach.

You, the reader, might want to think of how you would describe such family members or friends of yours.

HEALING SESSION:

Fr. Doria:

Before going into healing about feminine and masculine traits and roles, I want to read to you this apt passage from many centuries ago concerning what we are to believe as absolutely real and normative coming from the New Testament:

> From a homily on the first letter to the Corinthians by St John Chrysostom, bishop—
>
> The weakness of God is stronger than men.
> It was clear through unlearned men that the cross was persuasive,

in fact, it persuaded the whole world. Their discourse was not of unimportant matters but of God and true religion, of the Gospel way of life and future judgement, yet it turned plain, uneducated men into philosophers. How the foolishness of God is wiser than men, and his weakness stronger than men!...

Paul had this in mind when he said: *The weakness of God is stronger than men.* That the preaching of these men was indeed divine is brought home to us in the same way. For how otherwise could twelve uneducated men, who lived on lakes and rivers and wastelands, get the idea for such an immense enterprise? How could men who perhaps had never been in a city or a public square think of setting out to do battle with the whole world? That they were fearful, timid men, the evangelist makes clear; he did not reject the fact or try to hide their weaknesses. Indeed, he turned these into a proof of the truth. What did he say of them? That when Christ was arrested, the others fled, despite all the miracles they had seen, while he who was leader of the others denied him!

How then account for the fact that these men, who in Christ's lifetime did not stand up to the attacks by the Jews, set forth to do battle with the whole world once Christ was dead – if, as you claim, Christ did not rise and speak to them and rouse their courage? Did they perhaps say to themselves: "What is this? He could not save himself but he will protect us? He did not help himself when he was alive, but now that he is dead, he will extend a helping hand to us? In his lifetime he brought no nation under his banner, but by uttering his name we will win over the whole world?" Would it not be wholly irrational even to think such thoughts, much less to act upon them?

It is evident, then, that if they had not seen him risen and had proof of his power, they would not have risked so much. (August 24 – Office of Readings for St. Bartholomew)

Some of you might ask yourselves: Have I become so sophisticated in hermeneutics that I no longer see the path the Doctors of the Church saw so clearly?

Mostly, I thought it would be healing for you to take a look at this traits list. I know that this list is stereotypical, but just the same I have found it useful in workshops I give on the subject of feminine and masculine issues.

Fr. Doria handed out this page.

Both of you, women and men in this seminar go through all these traits, feminine and masculine and circle ones you think you usually display. Then go through all the POSITIVE traits of both sexes putting a box around ones you wish you manifested more often.

Positive Feminine Traits:

affectionate, caring, charming, compassionate, considerate, delicate, diplomatic, empathetic, enduring, expressive, faithful, friendly, gentle, gracious, hospitable, intuitive, kind, nurturing, perceptive, polite, pure, quiet, sincere, soft, supportive, sweet, tender, trusting, warm.

Negative Feminine Traits:

catty, chatter-box, complaining, (overly) curious, (overly) dependent, (overly) emotional, fearful, flirtatious, gossipy, grudging, hysterical, jumpy, manipulative, mean, moody, nagging, naive, passive, petty, pouty, prudish, seductive, (overly) sensitive, silly, slavish, smothering, spiteful, vain, weak, weepy, wishy-washy.

Positive Masculine Traits:

adventuresome, assertive, authoritative, brave, chivalrous, daring, decisive, determined, driving, firm, focused, forceful, initiating, just, leading, logical, objective, protective, prudent, self-controlled, sporty, steady, straightforward, strong, valiant.

Negative Masculine Traits:

(overly) ambitious, argumentative, blunt, brutal, callous, cold, competitive, condescending, dare-devil, domineering, hiding of feelings, inconsiderate, insensitive, isolated, lustful, plotting, proud, rude, ruthless, sarcastic, self-centered, smugness, task-oriented, territorial, uncaring.

After you have finished, pray about what you found. You might want to thank God for the good ones you have and repent of any negative ones. On those negatives, you might confess any that have hurt others. Especially consider negative traits that show themselves sometimes in your relationship to Catholics in other parts of the Spectrum.

When I, Ronda, did this exercise, I shamefully admitted that such negative feminine traits as cattiness, meanness, and spitefulness showed themselves in arguments with opponents on Church teachings. And, even more were negative masculine traits such as argumentativeness, bluntness, pride (wanting always to be proved right publicly), and sarcasm.

I decided to make my confession to Fr. Doria. Since he has known me for so many years, I wouldn't have to come up with any examples for him to know just what I meant. I also recalled Von Hildebrand contrasting the lax with the Pharisaical and saying that the self-righteous Pharisee loves to hurl denunciations from the throne of truth! Mea culpa!

When I confessed to loving one-upmanship and savoring perfect refutations of my opponents, Fr. Doria surprised me with by this advice. "Some people aren't ready for the truth, so no matter how well you express a truth they may not be able to accept it. But Jesus always wants us to desire to love others, including enemies or opponents. Ask Jesus to help you desire to love everyone in the other parts of the Spectrum."

During the night I woke up and remembered an image used by a spiritual teacher: "a moral flimsy." Something flimsy is weak and easily destroyed. The context in which one of my co-authors, Sister Mary Neill, O.P., used the term moral flimsy was this. A sinful person will often use excuses for his or her bad behavior. Another person, exasperated by the denial, then tries to demolish the excuses. That critic tries to tear off the "moral flimsy" of the sinner.

Here's the point. I, Ronda, exasperated by the denials involved in the theological opinions of my opponents on Catholic issues, want to tear off their "moral flimsy" through stinging sarcastic arguments!

But if I pray to desire to love them more…how much better.

Not that it isn't good for a philosopher and writer to advance good arguments for the truths of the faith, but always speaking the truth with love.

6.

DAY V

Economic Philosophy: Socialism vs. Modified Capitalism

Military Conflict: Peace vs. Just War

MORNING SESSION:

Fr. Doria: Most of the active saints through the ages were fiercely for the poor. But it is only fairly recently that parish Catholics thought about influencing the political scene in the way we now think of concerning social justice issues. With the advent of democracy, industrialism, capitalism, socialism, and communism, the Catholic in the pew certainly had opinions, and some became active in such movements as unionism, civil rights, struggling, or even revolution against repressive regimes, solidarity, and pro-life, to mention some especially prominent causes.

In my seminary training, I read with the greatest interest the Social Encyclicals of the Popes. It seems as if some on the Spectrum, while inveighing against such trends as liberation theology, are not as knowledgeable as one would hope about the Church's social justice valid teachings. For example, although Saint Pope John Paul II was fiercely critical of the communism under which he lived in Poland, he also wrote about the lesser but real evils of unchecked capitalism.

I was startled when Saint Mother Teresa of Calcutta on a visit to the United States remarked that while the social justice conferences here seemed to be bogged down in controversy, her own Sisters had taken care of 10,000 dying poor in Calcutta.

And somehow Catholics don't talk enough to others about the enormous works of care throughout the centuries, mostly for the poor of the Church, in hospitals and schools.

It is argued that while liberation theologians used to visit St. Oscar Romero, he was actually not one of them, even though he condemned repression of the poor by evil regimes.

Nevertheless, there is surely a great division in our Church today between those who think that a modified capitalism (with a safety net) is good vs. those who believe that only a government-controlled economy can overcome the still great disparity between the rich and the poor.

Presently, the issue of immigration has become the most controversial, pitting Catholics who affirm the greatest possible openness to immigrants on the basis that their bad governments have led to extreme poverty against those who insist controlled borders are a necessity for our economy.

So, here is your morning question:

How has your family background, your Catholic college and graduate education and your own research influenced your teachings on economic issues?

James: When I was a child and teen in Louisiana, there was no Republican party there! You either voted Democratic or you didn't vote!!! When I started college at St. Athanasius, most of the professors and students voted democratic on the basis, precisely, of that party's seeming closer to the social justice teachings of the Church.

It was only with Roe v. Wade that many Catholics I knew switched over to the Republican party as more pro-life, even if not as effective as wished. I, myself, however, was unable to switch allegiance from Democrat to Republican because of my conviction that Republicans are willing to accept exploitation of the poor by capitalist monopolies in this country and in countries all over the world.

Ronda: How different our backgrounds were. My parents being ex-Communist, fierce anti-Communists, taught us even as youngsters about the horrors of Stalin's totalitarian state. In the public schools of that time, the 1940's, we saw educational films lauding the genius of industrialization. That we had the highest standard of living of any country in the whole world because of capitalism was taught as self-evident.

However, by High School in the 1950's, the picture changed so much that our parents seemed to be the only ones who voted Republican! As a Catholic, in graduate school studying philosophy, socialism was usually considered a good option. I always had the impression, however, that socialism was flawed by the simple fact that without the incentive of profit the whole world would be like the Soviet Union. In such places there was less abject poverty than under the Czar, but such a terribly low standard of living that most everyone drowned their despair in drink every night of the week!

James: I don't teach social philosophy, but my overview is that every economic system has advantages and disadvantages given the fallen nature of man. If I visit the homes of most middle-class friends, I find them cluttered with thousands upon thousands of possessions that would signify success, but their teens are mostly on drugs!

Ronda: I agree, but is the remedy to live in countries where life is so drab that, for instance, in Russia I have read most women have no children at all, but an average of 20 abortions each! On the other hand, even though I vote Republican because of the abortion platform of the Democratic party, I chide some of my Republican friends for speaking as if the US is the good country in spite of our huge abortion record!

On the immigration issue, I find it paradoxical that Catholic people coming from countries where the abortion rate is much lower are dying to come to the US and put their children in public schools where they will learn that killing their babies is good!

I absolutely agree that exploiting the poor for capitalistic gain is wrong, but how can so many democrats act as if the 60,000,000 aborted babies since Roe v. Wade are nothing?

James: I don't.

On another topic, some Catholics who are against social welfare programs consider them to be simply ways for lazy people to avoid working. I had a friend who worked for a government assistance program. This is what he said: "I know that about ½ of the people on assistance are cheating on the system. For example, the day the assistance check arrives in the mailboxes in our ghetto areas, the drug-dealer males visit the single-parent family, get the mother to sign the check, cash it, and leave them still without necessities. So why do I continue at my job? Because I am working for the other ½."

Ronda: I remember hearing on the radio that in one State they had put in a program of actively making almost all people on assistance work and gradually get off government help.

To get to the immigration issue, I heard from a Catholic radio show man that he had personally gone down to the border to see what was really going on. He was told that more than ½ the so-called separated families were really children who had been given over to sex-traffickers in hopes they could live better economically here and later bring the whole family over!! And then there is the whole drug dealer problem with some immigrants. And they get free-medical in the US while many of our own poor don't qualify.

James: I am hoping some politicians come up with real solutions to all of these complicated immigration problems. I don't trust journalists much about such issues.

Ronda: Me, neither. I mean the fake news thing drives me crazy. How can we know what to think if we don't know which commentators have the real facts?

By the way, I thought you might like the way I taught the need to help the poor to my ethics classes.

"Suppose you were going to Wal-Mart to buy 6 t-shirts on sale. At the door you see a poor woman huddled with a baby crying in her arms. "I have no money to buy food and no milk left in my breasts, can you help me?"

"Wouldn't you buy 1 t-shirt and give the rest of your money to her?"

Now, here's the point, you could give some of the money you earn that you spend for luxuries to the starving in, say, Calcutta, by giving it to them through Mother Teresa's Sisters and Brothers.

You think, "yeah, sure, but probably the people who run the charity get most of the money as part of the overhead of their fundraisers."

"In India, Mother Teresa's Sisters don't even have toilet paper! Where's the overhead???"

(If this argument seems strong, consider sending money to Mother Teresa's Sisters and Brothers through their US headquarters - Missionaries of Charity, 335 E 145 St., Bronx, NY 10451. When I send contributions I append to the check "for the most starving people you serve in the world."

James: It is the teaching of Jesus and of the Church that our luxuries belong to the poor. But what is a luxury is too hard to define to spell it out from the pulpit. For a pianist, a piano isn't a luxury, or, for that matter, neither is a computer for a professor!

LUNCH:

Some of the comments around the table were these:

"I knew a professor of Chinese who had escaped from Mao's China. He said the usual statistics about massacres by the communist regime were way low. This made me think that it is a travesty that the Vatican has now accepted the bishops and priests who are in league with the communists instead of helping the persecuted underground Chinese Catholic Church."

"I recently joined the American Solidarity Party. It's a new party based on a humanistic, mostly Christian, philosophy that includes pro-life and social justice. Google it!"

"I was talking to an anesthesiologist from India about the scandals about bad conditions and wages in US owned companies hiring people there. His response was this: "You Americans have no idea about what life is like there. One teenage girl getting a low salary in a factory owned by one of your companies earns the only money that can be used to feed a whole family of starving people."

"The food we throw away into the garbage in the United States could feed the whole world!"

MASS:

At the Mass, Fr. Doria took up a collection to help provide tuition to poor students in Africa who are affiliated with St. Athansius University.

Fr. Doria's homily.

https://www.pexels.com/photo/priest-standing-on-a-podium-during-mass-2194355/

ADORATION:

During Adoration of the Holy Eucharist I prayed this way:

"Oh my Jesus, you had such a love for the poor. How sad it must make you when you see so many in developed countries wasting so much money and food. Please inspire us to do more for poverty and good social justice initiatives."

AFTERNOON SESSION:

Fr. Doria: This afternoon, I would like you to work together on whether pacifism is the only answer to violence or whether some version of the just war theory can be Christian.

Ronda: When I taught this subject in ethics, I found it helpful to distinguish between 2 types of pacifism:

Pacifism A – Given the enormous emphasis on peace in the words of Jesus, I have chosen to be a peace-maker. Any kind of taking of the life of another human being is a sin for me, even if the motive is self-defense. I reject capital punishment, and any war. I do not, however, think that those who chose to kill others in self-defense or in a war against aggressors are committing a sin.

Pacifism B – Holds that any killing of a human person is evil for any person, and especially for a Christian.

James: I have not had to make the choice of evading a draft in what others thought to be a just war, but if I had been, I am pretty sure I would have refused to fight. Just the same, I would not think all Christians who did kill were sinful. I agree with the theory that whereas in the time of Jesus there was no way any Jews or, later, Christians, could have won in any battle, once there were whole areas of the world governed by Christians, it was taught that killing in self-defense or defense of the country was licit.

Ronda: I actually had trouble with that when I first became a Catholic. I thought pacifism B was self-evident. What helped me understand Church teaching about self-defense and just wars was the concept that an unjust aggressor forfeits his/her life by such actions. An analogy could be that a driver who is spaced out on drugs cannot blame a safe driver from hitting his/her car to avoid being hit.

James: I do think that all Christians should work for peace in their personal lives and in society at large. How impressive it is to read of how Gandhi managed to dethrone the English colonialists through non-violent resistance. And how wonderful was Martin Luther King, to apply such principles to fighting of civil rights for his people!

Ronda: It seems to surprise some pro-lifers when I mention that heritage as part of why we chose to pray in front of abortion clinics, or block the doors vs. trying to bomb baby-killing abortuaries.

James: Just the same, isn't it contradictory when some pro-lifers still insist that capital punishment is right?

Ronda: I think that the original statement in the Catechism is good. It says that even if justified in the case of grave crimes, it is more merciful to forgive. But, it includes the clause where conditions such as life-time imprisonment mean that innocent people will still be protected from those convicted. Now, many say this is now the case world-wide. I doubt it. For one thing, accounts of prison conditions I have read stress the corruption of the guards.

Besides, how can the same Catholics who oppose the killing of the proven evil-doer still vote for those who allow the violence of abortion of totally innocent babies?

Now, back to just war theory, the Catechism, written after the advent of nuclear warfare does rule out indiscriminate bombing of civilians. So it is not only the intention but also the means that can be wrong.

DINNER:

Fr. Doria: At your tables, I think it would be useful to tell each other which of the wars you have read about or participated in would fall into the category of just in your estimation?

I said I thought it is very hard to know if one is relying on historical and biographical materials. So, for many of us, the conditions in the US at the time of English colonialism don't seem anything like those of the Europe of WWII, but if we were living then, it could be different.

Someone mentioned that Abraham Lincoln once admitted that without belief in God and an afterlife he could never sleep at the thought of all who died in the Civil War.

Several talked about the irony of Americans considering England to be an aggressor while at the same time justifying how we took over the lands of the Native Americans.

HEALING SESSION:

Fr. Doria: I was wondering what we could do with these topics this evening. After all, few professors of philosophy and theology commit sins of exploitation of the poor or of fomenting wars!

Then I thought it would be good to pray for healing of others who have been victims of such sins. But, also ourselves, if we, or family members, have been hurt through unjust economic situations, or the victims of war in terms of loss of life or life-long trauma.

I, Ronda, was surprised to realize that none of those hurtful situations applied to me except in the most trivial form as in having less new clothing than upper middle-class school girls. Praying about this increased my desire to express gratitude for all I have been given and to give even more time and money to the really poor when possible.

I gave our priests the night off since Fridays can be busy in their parishes, but if you wish, I can hear confessions at the end.

7.

DAY VI

Hope for the Church

Suggested Follow Ups

Fr. Doria: I am hoping that due to this seminar we will not be still divided in purgatory! Do you want to see in purgatory one "mansion" for those who watered down Catholic dogmatic and moral truth and another "mansion" for those who spoke the truth, but with hate?

(Laughter)

Pet peeve?

I would like to see these hateful sarcastic descriptions by Catholics about other Catholics expunged from your vocabularies. If you never say such words aloud or in your thoughts, or have never even heard them, be glad!

Commie lib vs. socialist

Lesbo or fairy vs. same-sex female attraction or same-sex male attraction

Cafeteria Catholics vs. doubting Catholics

Fanatics vs. militants

Old-fashioned pre-Vatican II dinosaurs vs. lovers of tradition

Now I would like to read to you an article I read just yesterday. I realize that even though it can sound like a Spectrum #3 – moderate, moderate, moderate document, not all moderates will agree with everything in it. Just the same, a lot of it will be salutary for all of us no matter where we place ourselves on my Spectrum!

"What Can Unite Us Catholics?

Anthony Esolen – writer in residence of Magdalene College

(Sunday, July 21, 2019)[1]

"Amidst our unfortunate and time-bound divisions as regards partisan politics, I wonder whether it is possible to come up with a set of fundamentals that all Catholics can agree upon. Here is my attempt:

---

[1] This column first appeared at the website The Catholic Thing (www.thecatholicthing.org). Copyright 2019. All rights reserved. Reprinted with permission. See https://thecatholicthing.org/2019/07/21/what-can-unite-us-catholics/

1. All the tenets of the Nicene Creed are true, without reservation or equivocation. The Father *is the Father*, from whom all fatherhood derives as from its originating fountain. It is no mere customary name. Human fatherhood is merely analogical by comparison. The Son is the co-eternal Word "through whom all things were made." The Holy Spirit proceeds co-eternally from the Father and the Son. The Word was incarnate of the Virgin Mary, and made man, to suffer and die *for us, and for our sins,* and he rose again, as all flesh will rise again.

2. The words of Jesus are prescriptive forever. They are never to be made merely relative to his place and time. When it comes to God, faith, good and evil, and man and his destiny, we are never to suppose that we know better than the Lord. For He is Our Lord. He is not to be patronized or demoted to historical greatness. He alone has "the words of everlasting life."

3. It is *not impossible* that Christ, who has flocks we may not know of, will save those who do not know they are being saved through the agency of His Church. It is not, however, to be presumed in the case of individuals or peoples. Evangelizing is imperative. "Go forth," says the Lord, "and make disciples of all nations."

4. The Lord has willed that we come to knowledge of Him by means of other human beings in general, and by the Church specifically. Therefore, we must resist all temptations to place the words and example of the Lord on one side, and the teachings of the apostles and of the Church on the other, as if in opposition, or

as if the letters of Saint Paul or the other apostolic writers might be denigrated or ignored.

5. The Church's teachings regarding sex, marriage, and family life are true, salutary, and liberating. They are discoverable by natural reason and by an unconstrained reading of Scripture and of the words of the Lord Himself. Sins against them are destructive of the person, the family, and the common good, and cause especially serious harm, material, social, and spiritual, to children and to the poor. Separation of husband from wife may in some cases be a necessary evil, as the amputation of a gangrenous limb may be, but it is nevertheless a great social evil even when it is morally permissible.

6. The command to assist the poor is absolute and personal. Every Catholic must be engaged in it. Material poverty may be first in the order of urgency, as a man dying of thirst needs a drink of water before he needs a sermon. But as the soul is greater than the body, so also moral, intellectual, and spiritual poverty is more dreadful than material poverty, and these too we are commanded to alleviate or remedy.

7. Human life *is sacred.* Innocent human life must never be taken intentionally. That includes our own lives. We are made in the image of God, and therefore, when we encounter any human life, we are on holy ground: we stand in the light of one for whom God made the world. Nor may we stand idly by while the sick and the hungry need our care, for what we do to "the least of these," the

sick, the dying, the homeless, the unborn child, we do to Christ
Himself.

9. All that we possess comes from God and is meant to serve and
glorify Him. Our bodies are not our own to dispense with as we
please. Our material wealth is not our own to dispense with as we
please. That is a fact of our existence: we are creatures. Such sinners
as we are must never forget it, for we have been "purchased at a
price."

9. As the Sabbath is the crown of the week, so all of our work
should be oriented toward the Sabbath, its joy and its rest, the glory
we give to God, and our coming together with other human beings
for the common good on earth and for a foretaste of the eternal
good to come. Work for work's sake is a form of that spiritual
sluggishness known as *acedia.*

10. The world of remunerative labor should be organized so as to
provide gainful employment to able-bodied or able-minded men,
with wages sufficient to support their wives and children in a
becoming way. This does not mean that women do not work. It
does mean that the first aim of a just social policy regarding work
and wages is the health of the household, for that is what the very
word *economy* implies.

11. As the yeast leavens the whole of the dough, so the Catholic
faith should leaven every feature of the Catholic school: as to what

is taught, how it is taught, and who teaches it. Catholic teachers must in their public lives be witnesses to the truths of the faith.

12. Worship is the solemn and joyful duty we owe to God. All features of the Mass must be oriented *ad Deum: Patrem et Filium et Spiritum Sanctum.* Worship that turns a congregation inward upon itself is deficient at least, even when undertaken with good intent. Mass must not be demoted to a social. "Seek first the kingdom of God," says the Lord. If we do not, we will be like those who have little, "and even the little they have will be taken away." For man is that sort of creature who is united only from above: our brotherhood depends upon our acknowledging the Fatherhood of God.

What about it, my fellow Catholics? Can we agree at least to these?"

Fr. Doria smiled. Of course I realize that not all of you agree with everything in this hopeful vision. Still, you may find some of the wording challenging in areas where you may be weak.

For follow-up to our Crisis in the Church seminar?

You might consider reading the catechism from cover and cover seeing what you might have missed the first time you read it.

You might ask others in the Spectrum, especially moderates, what writers they like best. For example, many who disagree on subjects we have been talking about find common ground in spirituality books such as those of Henri Nouwen.

At end of seminar Fr. Doria said: "If this helped you understand people on other parts of the spectrum of division, maybe Ronda, our participant who writes books the most quickly, could make this into a manual for ministry to other groups."

CLOSING MASS:

Fr. Doria: My guess is that you have heard more than you ever wanted to from me, so I am going to make this short and in the form of a prayer:

"Holy Spirit, we are part of Your Church. And Your Church is in crisis. Help us to glimpse the plan of love you have for us. May whatever is true in the concepts of any part of the Spectrum be expressed in such a way that all of us may be able to hear and become the more holy."

After the Our Father, at the time of the gesture of peace, Fr. Doria suggested that we extend a hand shake or embrace of peace all around the chapel with all the other participants.

That afternoon, on the Participant Evaluations of the Crisis in the Church Seminar, Fr. Doria read these comments from Ronda and James:

Ronda: I don't think that the divisions can be overcome. I think we more and more will be in different parishes depending on the priest's place on the spectrum. However, I learned from James Marley and others – I had fresh insight into some of the truths they hold dear. I learned that we don't have to hate each other, or view each other with sarcasm, but try to understand others better and pray for each other more.

James: It helped me understand all the anger better. In my classes, I think I will be able to present aspects of each of these issues with greater knowledge of the philosophies of the Church behind differing positions.

EPILOGUE

I wrote *The Crisis in the Church* in 2018. It is being published, however, at the end of 2020 and, surely, the year 2020 has exacerbated the tensions in the Church and in the US to a level unpredictable for many of us.

I mean, who would have thought that we would have a Presidential race between a Spectrum 1 or possibly 2 Catholic and a pro-life but not Catholic President running for a second term? And, at the same time, there would be a former Vatican official sending out his "proofs" that the election of Pope Francis was a fraud!

Since I am neither an expert in politics nor a canon lawyer, what I will put in this epilogue are excerpts from my journal of the year 2020 entitled *Home Free!*

I have chosen ones that touch on ways a Catholic might meet Jesus in these troubled times. Even though some of these are personal, and not directly related to the crises in Church and country, I think many of you readers can relate to them.

(from the Introduction)

Way back in the 1980's I wrote a poem with that Home Free theme:

How shall it be?
Shall those only reach heaven
who have hop-scotched
their way patiently toward the goal?
Or will you suddenly open Your arms
And cry out 'home free'?

(Oh, but first, as I always explain, words from the Lord, sometimes called locutions, are never to be taken as infallible. Since none of my hard-working spiritual directors through the years thought the one's I SEEM to get are erroneous, I leave it to the reader to decide if they come from Jesus or from my sub-conscious. I think they are from Jesus because they always, always, always seem to me better than my own thoughts.)

June 7, 2020

Ronda: Jumpy, up and down happy and uncertain about new plans to move into an apartment complex in Corpus Christi, Texas. Jesus, I surrender all this to You, You take over!

Jesus, Mary, Joseph: We are trying to bring you deeper into our hearts so you will not be picturing yourself so much being friendly with this person or that but reaching out to others from our arms.

Ronda: That sounds good. You know that I feel a little stuck. With the help of the Holy Spirit I have laid out to the tune of 77 books about spirituality including how I think God has led me to the truth about how to be holy. And yet, my latest mentor tells me that it is all there, but too intellectual. At this phase of my life, he believes I need to go much deeper, in a more contemplative direction.

Jesus: Run now, My beloved, into My wounds and hide there.

Ronda: For how long?

Jesus: Until you feel that peace I promised to my sons and daughters.

Ronda: This is good! Confusion is not of Jesus. Hence He invites me to hide in His wounds until it dissipates.

(In relation to the Crisis in the Church, we are often filled with confusion not knowing what voices to trust. When we hide in His wounds, we have a better sense of what we can do for the Church vs. feeling pushed and pulled by e-mail forwards insisting on one way or another of approaching the Crisis.)

(Words from a mentor): Now is the time to work for holiness. It is my belief that holiness is my little will totally commensurate in sync with

His Will. No sin there.

And as the Trinity is a union of love and love is of the will then holiness is a union of loving wills.

Your will = His Will.

Where love is, there is no sin. Hence, divine love in your heart equals holiness. This is what I am pointing you toward: Divine love.

Lastly, sanctity, holiness, heaven is a journey... from the mind to the heart. As you grow in Divine Love your mind is no longer the chief generator of spiritual activity for your soul. Rather it serves at the bidding of the heart under the administration of the Holy Spirit in His seven-fold Gifts. So then when your heart is finally full of Divine Love, which is infinite love, your life will be complete. You will have no will but to love! And you will be fully living in the Spirit when Jesus comes for you (1Thess. 5:23). Strive for THIS completion of your life's work and you will already be living the life of heaven on earth.

April 20, 2020

JESUS: That 12 Step tool, "Let go, let God," is an important theme for all of your bonds at this time of your life. Do it now. Every time you think of anyone you love among family and friends, pray to let go and let Me take care of them.

(I try to relate these words to fears about the Crisis in the Church.)

Ronda: A priest mentor told me that becoming more anxious in retirement could be because you don't get the esteem you had as a professor. You need more of God's love vs. trying for esteem.

(I am thinking that part of the anger involved in the Crisis in the Church is because we feel put down when those "on the other side of

the Church" won't agree with us.)
A person with whom I was in conflict concerning truths of the faith unexpectedly said "our love is deeper than any controversy."

April 24, 2020

Ronda: I watched a TV Mass and got so upset by what the priest said in the homily. He was talking about Gamaliel and said that as a leader he had learned to watch everything but rarely to intervene since usually bad things peter out. I immediately started thinking about tolerance and cover up of Church leaders and how it has hurt the Church.

Dear Holy Spirit, how should I react to such things? Should I only watch those who totally agree with me? But, then, I start getting annoyed by personality traits or the way their hair is cut!!!!

HOLY SPIRIT: It is part of the fallen nature of the world that things are often erroneously expressed, things are annoying or even evil. We have given you a good mind. You can notice something expressed in ways that can have bad effects without getting so upset. You can note this in your mind; not seek "symbolic victory" through denouncing it to your allies. Turn it into prayer, for example, for all the victims of leadership that was not vigilant enough. May your prayer be more heartfelt than your anger would have been.

Ronda: Jesus, why do I feel a little afraid?

Jesus: Whenever that wave of fear comes over you, grab My hand very tightly and hide in My heart.

May 6, 2020

Good talk with Gary McCabe, a mentor of mine, about trying to fix family members not back in the sacraments. He said:

Don't scheme.
Don't manipulate.
Don't goad.
Don't think of sarcastic rejoinders to their reluctance to do what is best.
Don't try to fix them.

Instead:

Love, pray, and surrender.

By grace something can change things for the better that you have no control over and could never even imagine.

If you do this you will have peace.

May 13, 2020

I was in an argument about ethics. I thought it was hopeless. The Holy Spirit seemed to tell me instead of arguing to listen to the cry and wounds underneath the proclamations of my opponent.

May 14, 2020

I think of the church as the celestial living room of Jesus to which He invites us and provides a heavenly dinner.

May 15, 2020

Need for clarification: A mentor uses the expression about God's love for us "He loves you just the way you are."

I take umbrage at that expression, as well as the adjective 'unconditional' about love. I think it may turn out to be a matter of semantics, but just to clarify:

> We can use the word love in many ways. I agree that God loves me and you and everyone in the sense of loving the unique created preciousness of each self without condition.

But, love is also used in the sense of approval. I love "your voice" means I think it is beautiful. I don't say "I love your voice" just as it is when you are singing a note flat!

And, in the same way, God doesn't love our sins and defects which are the enemies of our precious souls. And those sins and defects are part of us. When a parent says she or he loves her or his child, they don't mean they are pleased and happy with their children's sins and defects.

Now, I think that what this mentor meant in telling me that God loves me just as I am is that he doesn't want me to think that because of the sins I repent of and the defects I deplore that He doesn't love that self of mine, precisely as He sees me repenting and struggling. He doesn't want me to think all day:

Ronda – sinner and weak miserable wretch.

Instead, he wants me to think all day something more like "Ronda, in God's eyes, you are so dear and beautiful, struggling so hard and loving Me and My grace as I make you everyday a better vessel of My love."

However, since possibly half the Church members think of unconditional love as meaning that God loves us so much that He doesn't care if we miss Mass just to sleep in sometimes, or that we are homosexual lovers, or that we use contraception… I don't like to hear those words 'unconditional' and 'love you just as you are.'

Could we find some other word to use instead to convey that God doesn't despise and hate us because we are sinners and full of defects?

I would want to say to someone I was helping: Dear child of God, you need to believe much more strongly and feel much more strongly how much God loves you in spite of your sins and failings.

Jesus: About this matter think of Augustine's "hate the sin, love the sinner." I did not use euphemisms when speaking as a Prophet to the people. But, notice I totally forgave St. Paul for persecuting My

Church. Every sin or defect you see in people you must quickly pray for that person, ask for My help for them to change, and never speak about it until you feel love in your heart for them or to anyone else.

Ronda: Dear Mother Mary, please help me to pray for the grace to be humble every moment of the day in every circumstance.

Mother Mary: Your next step is to become more gentle. If you think of it as gentle that might be easier for you than the word humble. Be gentle with yourself in how you talk to yourself. Humor is good but self-castigation comes from pride. Transitions are hard for everyone but older people more so. Offer up for graces for your family members the things that make you anxious.

June 3, 2020

Ronda: I am wondering how well we forgive those who won't forgive us – precisely forgive them for not forgiving us, or seeming not to have!!!!

June 4, 2020

Ronda: Someone asked me about hatred. Here was my response:

Hatred is a very loose word. It can range from "I hate tutti-frutti ice-cream," to "I hate Hitler," to "I hate this family member who hurt me so much."

As you say, it can mean I wish this person would drop dead all the way to I can't forgive him/her to I just have bad feelings about so and so.

"Forgive and forget" is not in the Bible. No one can forget that so and so murdered my child, for instance.

However, even though we are not obligated to remain in friendship with those dangerous to ourselves or our loved ones, we still have to forgive.

If we are to forgive even enemies as bad as the torturers of Jesus in the Passion, to overcome the feelings of rage and of desire to punish or see punished, we must always forgive, pray for them to repent, pray for them to change, and be open to accepting them in former roles - as in we can't say, except in matters of life and death or being led into mortal sin, even if you repent I will never speak to you again and you can never cross the entrance to my house, etc. etc. etc. etc.

We should feel deep sadness that someone did something wrong that hurt us but also hurt his/her own self because of that sin.

On the other hand, we should never act as if others are sinners and we are always good. We cannot have God's forgiveness or that of others if we walk around full of pride in our own virtues.

How many forget that pride is a sin as well as sins of passion.

(Related to the *Crisis in the Church*, I am thinking of all those in the

Church who, while being basically pro-life, yet plan to vote for a party and its leaders who have the right to abort on their platform. Also, of those who so plan to vote in my family out of hatred of Trump. Even while trying to change their minds, I should not be filled with rage against them but forgive and pray.)

June 6, 2020

Ronda: Yesterday was an amazing day. I received a box that included old writings of family members, including the play my mother wrote about the splits in the Church after Vatican II. I didn't like the play at the time, but reading this play again after 4 decades, I saw that it had a lot that was right on about each side and some really great insights.

I realized that I have been living, in the 30 years since my mother's death, with a caricature of her in my mind in some important ways.

Here is a sample concerning love of enemies:

One character says: "The word love in time of war is intolerable to a patriot if it includes loving the enemy – whom we must hate or we could not fight him successfully."

Another character replies:

"Actually, there are times when we should hate. Can we fight evil unless we hate it? And evil is not an abstract thing. It is expressed in the actions of people.

"We are told to hate the sin and love the sinner – how many people can really separate the two?

"When you strike against evil, you strike the evil-*doer*.

"Even Jesus had to whip the money changers in the Temple. And those were pretty murderous words he used in describing the Pharisees. He did not temper his anger nor did he spare the sinners....

Another character: I suppose that is one reason why wars are possible. Each side must convince itself that the enemy represents something evil. Then one can strike with a good conscience.... It is never the sin that is killed in the process but the sinner, whom we claim to love... and the massacres go on and on, getting more merciless all the time."

NOW HERE IS THE KEY INSIGHT I AM PONDERING:

"Perhaps (there is a solution) only if we reverse the words and learn to say: *I love the sinner more than I hate the sin...*"

June 13, 2020

Ronda: Al Hughes, my spiritual director when I lived in Corpus Christi before, who will take that role on again when I return, said I should not use the word rejected or hate so much – too heavy. Someone may have other priorities and spend less or no time with me for a while – that doesn't mean he/she rejects me.

Distressing screaming rant I had about politics on the family prayer meeting.

Now, dear Jesus, in talking to someone else about this, I thought my scream, given the issue was about voting for pro-abort candidates, was like You whipping the money-changers in the Temple. Is that an excuse or really so?

Jesus: Even though I often felt called to upbraid some Pharisees and Sadducees, or the money-changers, that is not a reason why you, my human children, should speak the truth with raging hate.

June 21, 2020

Ronda: E-mail from Carla, my twin sister, after my rant:

Are we not "one body in Christ?" I will let go of anything hindering me from accepting you as you are, grieving though of our differences..."

August 12, 2020

Ronda: Oh, my Jesus, bridegroom of my heart and soul, I am so upset now about the Vigano crisis. Some think the whole thing revolves around the very soon coming of the end of time. What do You want me to think?

Jesus: I want you to think only that JESUS SAVES. I will save you and all whose hearts are right even if many have many misunderstandings of doctrine. Grab My hand and the hand of Mother Mary whenever you feel shaky.

Jesus: I told you that since you have given your all to the Church, when you need help in the future the Church will take care of you. Watch and see what comes up.

Ronda: During the prayer meeting I got the understanding that I am hopeful when I am in charge as in teaching and writing, but in my present life I am extremely pessimistic (melancholic) because I am not in control.

Holy Spirit: The more you let Us be in control the happier you will be.

October 23, 2020

Ronda: Sent to good leader friends:

Here is a new vocation for you: how would you like to facilitate a group called Schism-a-holics?

Symptoms:

- check favorite Catholic websites every hour minimum to see if Pope Francis has stepped down.

- check websites of favorite good guy Cardinals to see if they are doing anything symbolic of hopes to be elected at a conclave.

- check out every word the parish priest says for signs of which side of the schism he would be on if such should take place.

- try to manipulate savvy lay people on our side to start undercover communities with undercover priests if necessary.

Why do I have a feeling you wouldn't be excited to facilitate such a group on Zoom, say?...I can almost hear your laughter reading this!!!

October 28, 2020

Ronda: Got into a huge yelling rant at a family member over politics.

Jesus: Remember I was not a zealot. Talk the least about these subjects. The only way the world can be saved from sin is by conversion. So, even if it is good to vote the right way, I don't want you to be obsessing about the election. Whenever you feel critical of anyone, immediately pray for that person.

October 30, 2020

Ronda: After a nap I awoke with a sense of total failure because of the voting decisions of most members of my family.

Holy Spirit: I want to use that feeling to help you to see that you need to hide in the wounds of Jesus at this time of your life, and speak only what is given to you by Us, The Holy Trinity, and Mary, and Joseph and the angels and saints. I don't mean total silence about daily practical things, but concerning teaching others in general and the family in particular. Speak the truth with love, but avoid all argument.

Ronda: I woke up from a nap with this image in my head and made it into a poem to send to family members for Christmas:

A Together-Forever Family
 Not like a Flower Still-life
Tied in Place by Twine!

More like a kaleidoscope
Where bright colored glass
    pieces
Swirl into new places
New patterns

This Year some of you Moved
To New Places
Closer to some Bright Specks…
Further from Others.

Sometimes conflict seems
To push one of us off the page
But loving forgiveness

Seems always to bring us
Back together.

One Day
I will be Floating in Eternity
With Bright Colored
And you will have to
Look Upward to see me

Rays of Light will Join me,
I hope,
To the Bright Souls
Of each of you

In God
We will be, I hope,
Together
Forever.

(I have been reading a famous non-Catholic Christian mystic from Switzerland in the 19th century. Here is quote that I loved.)

> We are struck by something bewildering and ineffable when we look down into the depths of an abyss; and every soul is an abyss, a mystery of love and piety. A sort of sacred emotion descends upon me whenever I penetrate the recesses of this sanctuary of man, and hear the gentle murmur of the prayers, hymns, and supplications which rise from the hidden depths of the heart. These involuntary confidences fill me with a tender piety and a religious awe and shyness. The whole experience seems to me as wonderful as poetry, and divine with the divineness of birth and dawn. Speech fails me, I bow myself and adore. And, whenever I am able, I strive also to console and fortify.

Nov. 14, 2020

Ronda: I am reeling about the McCarrick report…dreaming of hiding in some underground Church with a group and priest I trust. I think You, my bridegroom, are telling me something else though????

Jesus: You want to fit everything that happens into little categories so you can dismiss them. I want, instead, to open your heart to full empathy with all the sufferings of others, especially those you know. You could be thinking about the sufferings of loneliness of those with same-sex-attraction. I want to fill that loneliness with My mystical love, or heal them so they can be open to the opposite sex's love and marriage, and also the comradely love of others of the same-sex.

So, now that you have so much time to pray, I want you to be in such communion with Me that you are not reeling but open, receptive, and loving.

Ronda: Yes. Amen. I surrender into Your hands my future life on earth and whatever you allow to happen in the lives of each of my beloved family members. Amen, amen, amen!

Ronda: Right after writing this, I found this verse in a hymn for today's Advent Office of Readings:

> "Daughter of Zion, rise
> To meet thy lowly King;
> Let not thy stubborn heart despise
> The peace he deigns to bring."

Do I secretly "despise" peace because of love of excitement? Drama queen vs. peaceful Christian?

Jesus: True peace is not dull boredom but a transcendent tender joy…I wish so much for you, my Ronda widow bride, to have such peace.

It doesn't matter where you will live or with whom. What matters is that inner grace.

www.ingramcontent.com/pod-product-compliance
Lightning Source LLC
Chambersburg PA
CBHW052110090426
42741CB00009B/1747